Activity Workbook

ExpressWays

Second Edition

S0-AFC-538

2

Steven J. Molinsky
Bill Bliss

Contributing Author
Dorothy Lynde

PRENTICE HALL REGENTS

A VIACOM COMPANY

Publisher: *Louisa B. Hellegers*
Electronic Production Editor: *Christine McLaughlin Mann*
Production Assistant: *Jennifer Rella*
Manufacturing Manager: *Ray Keating*

Electronic Art Production Supervisor: *Todd Ware*
Electronic Art Production Specialist: *Marita Froimson*
Art Director: *Merle Krumper*
Interior Design: *Ken Liao*

Illustrator: *Richard Hill*

The authors gratefully acknowledge the contribution of Tina Carver
in the development of the *ExpressWays* program.

© 1997 by PRENTICE HALL REGENTS
Prentice-Hall, Inc.
A Simon & Schuster Company
Upper Saddle River, New Jersey 07458

10   9   8   7   6

ISBN 0-13-570888-5

Prentice-Hall International (UK) Limited, *London*
Prentice-Hall of Australia Pty. Limited, *Sydney*
Prentice-Hall Canada Inc., *Toronto*
Prentice-Hall Hispanoamericana, S.A., *Mexico*
Prentice-Hall of India Private Limited, *New Delhi*
Prentice-Hall of Japan, Inc., *Tokyo*
Simon & Schuster Asia Pte. Ltd., *Singapore*
Editora Prentice-Hall do Brasil, Ltda., *Rio de Janeiro*

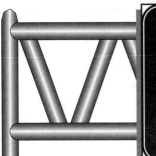

EXPRESSWAYS 2
Activity Workbook
TRAVEL GUIDE

Exit 3 • Food

Exit 4 • Personal Finances

Exit 5 • At Work

Exit 6 • Rules and Regulations

Exit 1

Greet Someone and Introduce Yourself

A. Wrong Way!

Put the lines in the correct order.

____ Brazil. And you?

____ Hi. I'm Teresa. Nice to meet you.

____ France.

__1__ Hello. I'm your new neighbor. My name is Louis.

____ Nice meeting you, too. Tell me, where are you from?

B. What's the Response?

Choose the correct response.

1 Where are you from?
   a. My apartment.
   b. Japan.

2 Who did she go with?
   a. To Chicago.
   b. Her neighbor.

3 When did you start your classes?
   a. I started History and English.
   b. I started last week.

4 How are you?
   a. Nice to meet you.
   b. Fine. And you?

5 Who is going to baby-sit?
   a. Jennifer.
   b. Saturday.

6 What does Maria study?
   a. On Monday and Wednesday.
   b. Chinese.

7 Why are you in this class?
   a. I have to learn English.
   b. I have a broken leg.

8 What's your major?
   a. Biology.
   b. Belgium.

9 What floor do you live on?
   a. The 7th.
   b. Apartment 7D.

10 Where are you going?
   a. On Tuesday.
   b. To my apartment.

11 Which apartment do you live in?
   a. 302.
   b. 472-3519.

12 Why can't you go to the movies with us?
   a. I can't go to the movies with you.
   b. I have to do my homework.

1

A. The Right Choice

Circle the correct word.

A. Excuse me. I'm new here. **Do** / (**Can**)[1] I ask you a question?

B. Sure.

A. **Is** / **Are**[2] there a park in this **neighbor** / **neighborhood**[3]?

B. Yes. **There's** / **It's**[4] a park around the corner.

A. Around the corner?

B. **No** / **Yes**[5].

A. That's great. Thanks very much.

B. Matching Lines

Match the questions and answers.

_c_ **1** Can I ask you a question?   a. At about 8:30.

____ **2** Where does the superintendent live?   b. Yes, I do.

____ **3** What time does the bus get here?   c. Sure.

____ **4** Is there a laundromat nearby?   d. Yes, I am.

____ **5** Are you happy in your neighborhood?   e. No, they don't.

____ **6** Where's the supermarket?   f. Yes, there is.

____ **7** Does Sally drive to work every day?   g. It's down the block.

____ **8** Do they pick up the garbage today?   h. No. She takes the bus.

____ **9** Do you like your new apartment?   i. He lives in the basement.

A. The Right Choice

Circle the correct word.

A. ((Can) Do)**¹** I leave my bicycle here?

B. Yes, you (can   can't)**²**.

A. (Do   Can)**³** I put my garbage here?

B. (No   Yes)**⁴**, you can't.

B. Listen

Listen and circle the word you hear.

1	can	(can't)	4	can	can't	7	can	can't
2	can	can't	5	can	can't	8	can	can't
3	can	can't	6	can	can't	9	can	can't

C. Sense or Nonsense?

Do the following "make sense" or are they "nonsense"?

		Sense	*Nonsense*
1	"You can go to the laundromat on the corner."	✔	
2	"You can play ball with your friends on the balcony."		
3	"The superintendent lives in the yard."		
4	"You can't leave your bicycle in the hallway."		
5	"You can hang your laundry in the fireplace."		
6	"You can plant flowers in the garden."		
7	"You can park your car in the garbage."		
8	"The bus stop is on the fifth floor."		

3

Offer to Help Someone

A. Wrong Way!

Put the lines in the correct order.

___ No, not at all.

___ Please. Let me help you.

_1_ Can I help you clean up this mess?

___ Thanks. I appreciate it.

___ Well, all right. If you don't mind.

___ No. That's okay. I can clean it up myself.

B. Listen

Listen and circle the word you hear.

1. (it)   them
2. it   them
3. it   them

4. it   them
5. it   them
6. it   them

7. it   them
8. it   them
9. it   them

C. Fill It In!

Fill in the correct answer.

1. Can I _____ you a question?
   a. ask
   b. use

2. Where can we _____ our laundry?
   a. plant
   b. hang up

3. Please. Let me _____ you.
   a. mind
   b. help

4. Can I _____ here in the yard?
   a. play ball
   b. use my fireplace

5. Excuse me. Where can I _____ my garbage bags?
   a. put
   b. pick up

6. Here. Let me help you _____ these tables.
   a. cut down
   b. put away

7. Thank you very much. I really _____ your help.
   a. thank
   b. appreciate

D. Word Search

Find the following words.

put away	take out	cut down	pick up	hang up	clean up

```
R  I  P  D  G  C  L  O  U  T  S  I  F  Z  B  B  O  P
C  L  E  B  A  C  J  Y  L  X  W (C  U  T  D  O  W  N)
D  O  K  E  Q  Z  A  C  T  P  R  A  W  L  N  C  M  E
T  U  P  I  C  K  U  P  A  N  S  V  P  T  N  P  K  A
C  L  O  P  X  E  P  T  A  F  P  U  P  V  P  L  Z  E
L  Y  W  R  Y  O  P  G  H  I  S  F  H  K  Z  C  B  M
E  Q  E  T  U  U  P  A  A  I  P  U  T  A  W  A  Y  P
A  D  G  J  K  R  L  X  N  N  E  T  U  O  S  P  A  G
N  K  L  D  R  H  Y  N  G  L  Z  W  Y  O  N  C  P  C
U  C  L  T  A  K  E  O  U  T  O  W  P  A  W  A  E  J
P  U  T  W  R  C  L  U  P  S  P  W  R  D  E  W  A  P
```

E. Listen

Listen and decide what these people are talking about.

1. (your bags)   your laundry
2. the mess   the bags
3. the laundry   the tree
4. the garbage   the mess
5. the table   the chairs
6. your things   your laundry

F. Wrong Way!

Put the words in the correct order.

1. _____ I can hang it up myself. _____
   it   hang   I   myself.   up   can

2. _____
   ourselves.   We   it   can   up   clean

3. _____
   right   up   Please   them   away.   pick

4. _____
   up   can   He   put   himself.   it

A. What's the Line?

Put a check next to the correct line.

1. Could I ask you a favor?

   ___ Fine. And you?
   ✔ What is it?

2. Could you lend me your car to pick up my son?

   ___ What is it?
   ___ All right.

3. Are you sure?

   ___ Yes. I'm not going to lend you my car.
   ___ Yes. I'd be happy to lend you my car.

   Thanks. I appreciate it.

B. Matching Lines

Match the lines.

_d_	1	Alice can't find the bus stop.
___	2	My friend and I don't have any money.
___	3	Betty wants to fix a table.
___	4	Tuesday is their anniversary.
___	5	Please write me a letter.
___	6	These shopping bags are heavy.
___	7	My English homework is difficult.
___	8	My friends and I love to listen to Mrs. Stoller.
___	9	Mr. Blaney can't start his car.
___	10	The Smiths are going to Rio next week.

a. Can you help me with it?

b. Could you help me carry them?

c. We can pick up their mail.

d. Can you help her find it?

e. Let's lend her a hammer.

f. We can help him start it.

g. Let's send them some flowers.

h. Could you lend us some?

i. Let me give you my address.

j. She tells us wonderful stories about her life.

A. The Right Choice

Circle the correct word.

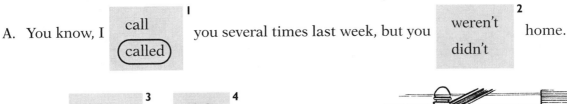

A. You know, I [call / **called**] ^1 you several times last week, but you [weren't / didn't] ^2 home.

B. No, I [didn't / wasn't] ^3 . I [did / was] ^4 in San Francisco.

A. Oh. What [were / did] ^5 you do there?

B. I [see / saw] ^6 a wonderful play.

A. Oh. That's nice.

B. Listen

Listen and circle the word you hear.

1	ring	(rang)	**9**	saw	called
2	have	had	**10**	were	weren't
3	was	wasn't	**11**	stopped	stop
4	drive	drove	**12**	took	look
5	come	came	**13**	do	did
6	did	didn't	**14**	went	sent
7	went	want	**15**	were	weren't
8	heard	read	**16**	read	saw

7

C. What's the Word?

Complete the sentences.

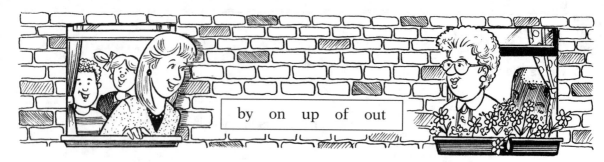

| by | on | up | of | out |

1. Could you take care _of_ my children this morning?

2. I took ____ the garbage for you.

3. We picked ____ the mail.

4. Please stop ____ my house today.

5. I came ____ yesterday, but you weren't home.

6. I knocked ____ your door.

7. We cleaned ____ the mess.

8. Please help me hang ____ the laundry.

D. What's the Response?

Choose the correct response.

1. Where did you go?
   (a.) I went to work.
   b. I go to work.

2. Why weren't you home?
   a. I wasn't at home.
   b. I was at the supermarket.

3. Who rang the doorbell?
   a. My neighbor rings the doorbell.
   b. My neighbor rang the doorbell.

4. How did you find out about the storm?
   a. I heard it on the radio.
   b. I was on the radio.

5. Did they see a movie yesterday?
   a. Yes. They see a funny comedy.
   b. Yes. They saw a funny comedy.

6. How did you go to the airport?
   a. I drove.
   b. I drive.

7. Did your friend stop by yesterday?
   a. Yes. He stop by at about 6:00.
   b. Yes. He stopped by at about 6:00.

8. Did you clean your apartment today?
   a. Yes, I did.
   b. Yes, I was.

9. Were you at home last week?
   a. No, I didn't. I was in Dallas.
   b. No, I wasn't. I was in Dallas.

10. I went to Los Angeles last week.
    a. Did you visited your cousins?
    b. Did you visit your cousins?

11. What did you do over the weekend?
    a. Nothing special. I was at home.
    b. Nothing special. I did at home.

12. Were you at school this morning?
    a. No, I didn't.
    b. No, I wasn't.

13. Do you want to see the mail?
    a. No, thanks. I saw it already.
    b. No, thanks. I see it already.

14. Was your homework difficult?
    a. No, it weren't.
    b. No, it wasn't.

Give Advice to Someone

A. Wrong Way!

Put the lines in the correct order.

___ I see. And you're trying to fix it yourself?

___ Hmm. You're probably right.

___ I'm trying to fix my stove.

___ What's wrong with it?

_1_ What are you doing?

___ It doesn't work.

___ Yes. But I'm having a lot of trouble.

___ You know, maybe you should call the gas company.

B. Listen

Listen to the conversation and choose the correct answer.

1.
  a. The woman is trying to fix a radiator.
  b. The woman fixed the radiator.

2.
  a. The radiator is leaking.
  b. The radiator doesn't get hot.

3.
  a. The woman is having a lot of trouble.
  b. The woman isn't having a lot of trouble.

4.
  a. Maybe she should call the superintendent.
  b. Maybe she should call a plumber.

C. The 5th Wheel!

Which one doesn't belong?

1. plumber	sink	electrician	carpenter
2. toilet	radiator	stove	electrician
3. supermarket	superintendent	apartment	floor
4. around the corner	down the block	in the basement	on Main Street
5. take out	take care of	put away	clean up

9

D. Crosswalk

| electrician | carpenter | plumber | superintendent | gas company |

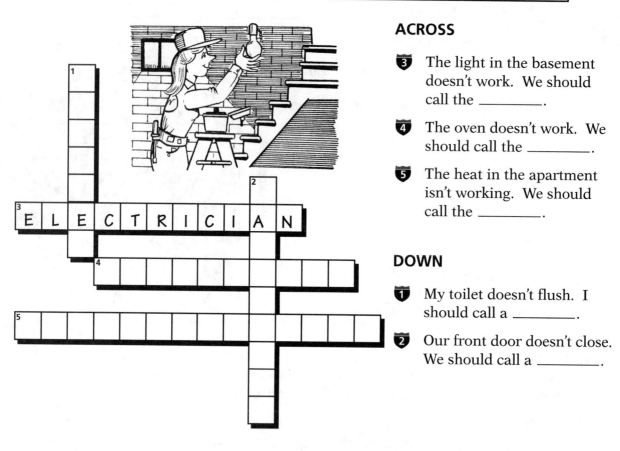

ACROSS

3 The light in the basement doesn't work. We should call the _____.

4 The oven doesn't work. We should call the _____.

5 The heat in the apartment isn't working. We should call the _____.

DOWN

1 My toilet doesn't flush. I should call a _____.

2 Our front door doesn't close. We should call a _____.

(Crossword grid: 3 Across reads E L E C T R I C I A N)

E. A Good Idea or Not A Good Idea?

Decide if each of these is a good idea or is not a good idea.

		A Good Idea	Not a Good Idea
1	"My sink is leaking. I'm going to call a plumber."	✓	
2	"This light doesn't work. I'm going to fix it myself."		
3	"My car doesn't start. I'm going to call Al's Garage."		
4	"My doorbell is broken. I'm going to call the gas company."		
5	"My fireplace doesn't work. I'm going to call the superintendent."		
6	"My stove doesn't go on. I'm going to fix it with a hammer."		
7	"My toilet doesn't flush. I'm going to call an electrician."		
8	"My radiator doesn't get hot. I'm going to put it on the balcony."		

10

A. What's the Line?

Choose the correct lines.

1 ELECTRICIAN: Tally's Wiring Company.

CUSTOMER: a. Hello. Do you fix broken doorbells?
b. Hello. Are there broken doorbells?

2 ELECTRICIAN: Yes. What's the problem?

CUSTOMER: a. My doorbell is leaking.
b. My doorbell doesn't ring.

3 ELECTRICIAN: I see. We can send an electrician at four o'clock this afternoon. Is that okay?

CUSTOMER: a. Four o'clock this afternoon? Yes, I'm fine.
b. Four o'clock this afternoon? Yes, that's fine.

4 ELECTRICIAN: Okay. What's the name and the address?

CUSTOMER: a. The name is Beth Miller, and the address is 57 White Street.
b. The name is 57 White Street, and the address is Beth Miller.

5 ELECTRICIAN: Phone number?

CUSTOMER: a. 57 White Street.
b. 468-2907.

6 ELECTRICIAN: All right. An electrician will be there at four o'clock this afternoon.

CUSTOMER: a. Thank you.
b. That's nice.

B. Listen

Listen and decide what these people are talking about.

1	kitchen sink	front door	**5**	toilet	front door
2	light	toilet	**6**	refrigerator	dishwasher
3	refrigerator	radiator	**7**	car	stove
4	stove	sink	**8**	refrigerator	radiator

C. Analogies

| took | mess | ran | cousins | saw | electrician | sat | weren't |

1. sink : plumber *as* light switch : ___electrician___
2. drive : drove *as* sit : _____
3. grandchild : grandchildren *as* cousin : _____
4. get : got *as* run : _____
5. have : had *as* see : _____
6. was : wasn't *as* were : _____
7. take out : garbage *as* clean up : _____
8. hear: heard *as* take : _____

D. Open Road!

What did you do when something in your home was broken?

When my .... didn't work, I ....

....

E. WordRap: *Home Emergencies*

Listen. Then clap and practice.

A. Quick! Call the plumber!
   Call him today!
B. What should I tell him?
   What should I say?
A. Tell him to hurry!
   Tell him to rush!
   The sink is leaking
   And the toilet doesn't flush!
   Tell him to hurry!
   Tell him to rush!
   The sink is leaking
   And the toilet doesn't flush!

A. Call the electrician!
   Call her today!
B. What should I tell her?
   What should I say?
A. Nothing's working!
   Nothing's right!
   The lights come on
   In the middle of the night!
   Nothing's working!
   Nothing's right!
   The lights come on
   In the middle of the night!

A. What's the Word?

Complete the conversation.

Dial	number	area code	"one"	call

A. Excuse me. Could you please tell me how to make a long-distance ___call___ **1**?

B. Sure. _____ **2** "one." Dial the _____ **3**. Then, dial the local _____ **4**. Have you got that?

A. I think so. Let me see. I dial _____ **5**. I dial the _____ **6**. And then I . . . hmm. Could you repeat the last step?

B. Yes. Dial the local _____ **7**.

A. Okay. I understand. Thanks very much.

B. Matching Lines

Match the lines.

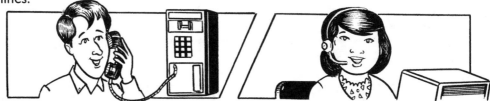

_d_ **1** Pick up ____.

____ **2** Put the money ____.

____ **3** Give the name of the person ____.

____ **4** Could you tell me how to use ____?

____ **5** Tell the operator it's a collect ____.

____ **6** Could you tell me how to make ____?

____ **7** Dial the area code and the local ____.

____ **8** Dial ____.

a. this pay phone

b. "zero"

c. in the coin slot

d. the receiver

e. number

f. you're calling

g. call

h. a person-to-person call

C. Listen

Listen to the conversation. Check the directions you hear.

Box 1:

✔ Dial "zero."

___ Put money in the coin slot.

___ Dial the area code and the local number.

___ Tell the operator it's a collect call.

___ Ask the operator's name.

___ Give your name.

Box 2:

___ Pick up the receiver.

___ Dial "zero."

___ Put the money in the coin slot.

___ Dial the number.

___ Put down the receiver.

___ Tell the operator your name.

Box 3:

___ Dial "zero."

___ Put the money in the coin slot.

___ Dial the area code and the local phone number.

___ Tell the operator it's a person-to-person call.

___ Give the operator your name.

___ Give the name of the person you're calling.

D. Open Road!

Who do you usually call on the telephone?

Person I call	Local phone call?	Long-distance call?	International call?	Collect call?	Person-to-person call?
My friend Bob	no	yes	yes	no	sometimes

A. Wrong Way!

Put the lines in the correct order.

___ What's your name?

___ All right. One moment, please.

_1_ Operator.

___ No. Sally Zeltzer.

___ Sally Zeltzer.

___ I want to make a collect call, please.

___ Did you say "Sally Seltzer"?

B. Listen

Listen and put a check next to the sentence you hear.

1 ___ Is this Larry's Department Store?
   ✔ Is this Lally's Department Store?

2 ___ Do you have any beaches?
   ___ Do you have any peaches?

3 ___ Did you call at seven?
   ___ Did you call at eleven?

4 ___ I fixed the drain.
   ___ I fixed the train.

5 ___ Is the museum open late?
   ___ Is the museum open at eight?

6 ___ I think you're right.
   ___ I think you're light.

7 ___ The collect call was from my father.
   ___ The collect call was from my brother.

8 ___ Do you sell bears?
   ___ Do you sell pears?

9 ___ Is your name Hal?
   ___ Is your name Al?

10 ___ Are you calling Mr. Leardon?
   ___ Are you calling Mr. Reardon?

11 ___ They sell gold watches.
   ___ They sell cold watches.

12 ___ What's the address of the store?
   ___ What's the address on the door?

13 ___ Please come at three.
   ___ Please come and see.

14 ___ Is there a problem with your hearing?
   ___ Is there a problem with your earring?

15

A. What's the Response?

Choose the correct response.

1. May I please speak to Mr. Rodriguez?
   a. I'm sorry. He isn't here right now.
   b. Will he be back soon?

2. Mrs. White isn't in. She'll be back in a few hours.
   a. Okay. I'll call back then.
   b. Will she be back soon?

3. When will Emily be back?
   a. I'll call her when she gets back.
   b. She won't be back until 5:00.

4. This is Jim Daniels calling.
   a. Nice meeting you.
   b. Do you want to leave a message?

5. Do you want to leave a message for Louise?
   a. Yes. Please ask her to call me.
   b. I want to talk to Louise.

6. Ben isn't here right now.
   a. Is Ben there?
   b. Oh, I see. When will he be back?

7. Will Mrs. Ferguson be back soon?
   a. She isn't here right now.
   b. She'll be back in a few minutes.

8. Please ask Tom to call me when he gets back.
   a. All right.
   b. Thank you.

9. I'll give them the message.
   a. Okay. I'll call back then.
   b. Thank you.

10. May I ask who's calling?
   a. I'm calling Fred.
   b. This is Anita Lane.

B. WordRap: *Trouble Getting Through!*

Listen. Then clap and practice.

I called Dr. Brown,
But he was out of town.
I called Aunt Lizzie,
But her line was busy.
I called Uncle Fred,
But the line went dead.
I called Irene
And got her answering machine.

I placed a long-distance call
To a friend in Bombay,
And got a machine
That said, "Have a nice day!"

C. Likely or Unlikely?

Is it "likely" or "unlikely" that someone would say the following?

Mr. Drayton will be back in fifteen years.

		Likely	*Unlikely*
1	"Mr. Drayton will be back in fifteen years."	_____	✓
2	"Please ask Michael to call me when he gets back."	_____	_____
3	"May I please speak to me?"	_____	_____
4	"Mrs. Mazer will be back from lunch in a few days."	_____	_____
5	"This is Bob's dog calling."	_____	_____
6	"I'll give her the message next month."	_____	_____
7	"Please ask her to call me tomorrow."	_____	_____
8	"The electrician will be there after lunch."	_____	_____
9	"The plumber will be there at 2:00 in the morning."	_____	_____
10	"Ramon won't be back from his English class until sometime next year."	_____	_____

D. Matching Lines

Match the questions and answers.

_f_ **1** Will Janet be back soon?		a. Yes, you will. You'll get a raise in March.
____ **2** Will the bus be on time?		b. Yes, I will. I'll call him after 7:00.
____ **3** Will Mr. and Mrs. Murayama be here soon?		c. Yes, she will. She'll call him at 10:30.
____ **4** Will you call your friend tonight?		d. No, it won't. It'll be cloudy all day.
____ **5** Will Edward call you collect?		e. Yes, we will. We'll be home all evening.
____ **6** Will I get a raise this year?		f. No, she won't. She won't be back until 6:00.
____ **7** Will it be sunny tomorrow?		g. No, it won't. The bus will definitely be late.
____ **8** Will Margaret call her son this morning?		h. No, he won't. He won't call me collect.
____ **9** Will the mail come soon?		i. Yes, it will. The mail will come at noon.
____ **10** Will you and your wife be home tonight?		j. Yes, they will. They'll be here at ten.

A. The Right Choice

Circle the correct word.

A. | What^1 / (When) | is the next bus to Houston?

B. It's at | $11.55 / 11:55 |^2 .

A. At | 11:55 / $11.55 |^3 .

B. Yes.

A. I'd like a round-trip | bus / ticket |^4 , please.

B. All right. That'll be eighteen dollars and fifteen cents | ($18.15) / (18:15) |^5 .

B. Listen

Listen and complete the train schedule.

TRANSAMERICA RAIL SERVICE			
Destination	One-Way Fare	Round-Trip Ticket	Leaves
New York	———	$64.00	10:10 A.M.
Philadelphia	$43.80	———	———
Washington	$52.00	———	6:48 P.M.
Atlanta	———	$122.30	11:05 A.M.

18

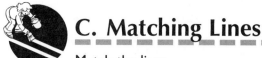

C. Matching Lines

Match the lines.

_f_ **1** A noise woke us ____ .

____ **2** We usually eat lunch at ____ .

____ **3** The sun goes down ____ .

____ **4** I usually get home from work at ____ .

____ **5** The sun usually comes up ____ .

____ **6** I usually go to bed at ____ .

a. 6:00 in the evening

b. midnight

c. noon

d. at about 5:45 in the morning

e. at around 7:30 in the evening

f. at 2:00 in the morning

D. What's the Response?

Choose the correct response.

1 How much is the ticket?
   a. It's $10.25.
   b. It's 10:25.

2 Where does this bus go?
   a. To Baltimore.
   b. At 9:30.

3 When does the flight to Cairo leave?
   a. It's $114.50.
   b. At 11:45 A.M.

4 What time does Train 57 arrive in Toronto?
   a. It arrives at 12:08.
   b. I arrive at 12:08.

5 Where did you go on vacation?
   a. I go to London.
   b. I went to London.

6 How did you get there?
   a. On Tuesday.
   b. By boat.

7 How much is a one-way ticket to Philadelphia?
   a. It's $275.00.
   b. Which do you prefer?

8 I'd like a round-trip ticket to San Diego.
   a. Is it a round-trip ticket?
   b. Okay. That'll be $87.75.

9 How do you usually travel long-distance?
   a. By collect call.
   b. By plane.

10 When is the next plane to Beijing?
   a. It won't leave soon.
   b. At midnight.

11 How many tickets do you want?
   a. Four tickets, please.
   b. Round-trip, please.

12 Do you prefer the train or the plane?
   a. Yes, I do.
   b. The train.

Understand Transportation Safety Rules

A. Unscramble and Match

Unscramble the sentences below. Then match them with the appropriate scene.

___

1

___

___

___

___

1 _Please don't lean against the doors!_

the   don't   Please   doors!   against   lean

2 _____

cars!   between   don't   Please   the   ride

3 _____

belt!   your   seat   fasten   Please

4 _____

don't   bus!   on   radio   Please   your   the   play

5 _____

behind   line!   the   Please   white   stand

6 _____

the   you!   of   your   under   bag   seat   Please   in   put   front

20

B. What's the Word?

Complete the sentences.

between	under	in front of
behind	on	against

1 The flowers are ___on___ the table.

2 The chair is _____ the fireplace.

3 The purse is _____ the table.

4 The son is leaning _____ the door.

5 The dog is _____ the chair.

6 The daughter is standing _____
her mother and father.

C. Sense or Nonsense?

Do the following "make sense" or are they "nonsense"?

		Sense	*Nonsense*
1	"Please don't stand on that chair!"	✓	_____
2	"Please stand with the white line!"	_____	_____
3	"Stand in front of the building!"	_____	_____
4	"Put your book between the chair!	_____	_____
5	"Please sit under me!"	_____	_____
6	"Put the money behind the coin slot!"	_____	_____
7	"Stand on your son!"	_____	_____
8	"Please go to the store with your brother!"	_____	_____
9	"Please don't lean against the door!"	_____	_____
10	"Please fasten your seat bag!"	_____	_____
11	"Don't ride your bicycle on the expressway!"	_____	_____
12	"Please don't go out tonight!"	_____	_____
13	"Please put away those dishes!"	_____	_____
14	"Put the cake under the children!"	_____	_____
15	"Make a collect call!"	_____	_____
16	"Please don't lean in front of you!"	_____	_____

A. Wrong Way!

Put the lines in the correct order.

___ Did you say Sixth and Seventh Avenue?

___ I want to report an emergency!

___ Where?

___ All right. We'll be there right away.

_1_ Police.

___ What's your name?

___ A man just had a heart attack.

___ Yes. That's right.

___ Michael Chen.

___ On Main Street, between Sixth and Seventh Avenue.

___ Yes. Go ahead.

B. Unscramble the Messages!

Put the following emergency messages in the correct order.

1 _____ A car just hit a pedestrian. _____
a   pedestrian.   A   hit   just   car

2 _____
jogger   the   Somebody   mugged   in   a   park.

3 _____
Street.   a   accident   Main   There's   bad   on

4 _____
just   a   store.   Somebody   department   robbed

5 _____
had   heart   A   just   attack.   woman   a

C. What's the Word?

Complete the story.

left	ate	took	woke	saw	sat	went	got

Bill and Melissa _____went_____ ¹ to the mall last Saturday to buy a birthday present for their son Tommy. Tommy was going to be three years old on Sunday, and they wanted to buy him a special present. They _____ ² up early and _____ ³ their apartment at 8:30 A.M. They _____ ⁴ a bus to the mall. They _____ ⁵ many wonderful presents for Tommy. There were books, balls, and toy cars. But they really liked the toy trains, and so that's what they _____ ⁶ him. For lunch, they went to a restaurant in the mall and _____ ⁷ Italian food. After lunch, they _____ ⁸ at the table and planned Tommy's birthday party.

D. What's the Question?

Complete the conversation.

How did you get there?	What did you do there?	I'm sorry. What did you say?
Where did you go?	Who did you go with?	What time did the plane leave?

1. _____Where did you go_____? I went to Brazil.
2. _____? I went by plane.
3. _____? I said I went by plane.
4. _____? I went with my husband.
5. _____? At 2:30 in the afternoon.
6. _____? We saw beautiful mountains and beaches.

23

Tell the Quantities of Food You Need to Buy

A. Matching Lines

Match the lines.

_c_	**1**	Let's buy a bottle of ____.	a.	bananas
___	**2**	Let's get a bunch of ____.	b.	eggs
___	**3**	We need to buy a gallon of ____.	c.	ketchup
___	**4**	We need a dozen ____.	d.	milk

___	**5**	Let's get two bags of ____.	e.	butter
___	**6**	We need a pound of ____.	f.	potato chips
___	**7**	Let's buy a box of ____.	g.	orange juice
___	**8**	We need to get a quart of ____.	h.	cookies

___	**9**	Please get a pint of ____.	i.	grapes
___	**10**	We need a jar of ____.	j.	whole wheat bread
___	**11**	Can you get a loaf of ____?	k.	ice cream
___	**12**	Please buy a bunch of ____.	l.	mayonnaise

B. The 5th Wheel!

Which one doesn't belong?

1	milk	lettuce	eggs	butter
2	skim milk	orange juice	rice	apple juice
3	ketchup	apples	oranges	grapes
4	chocolate ice cream	vanilla ice cream	cookies	tuna fish
5	apples	eggs	milk	potato chips
6	quart	half a gallon	half a dozen	gallon
7	jars	quarts	loaves	bottles

C. Crosswalk

ACROSS

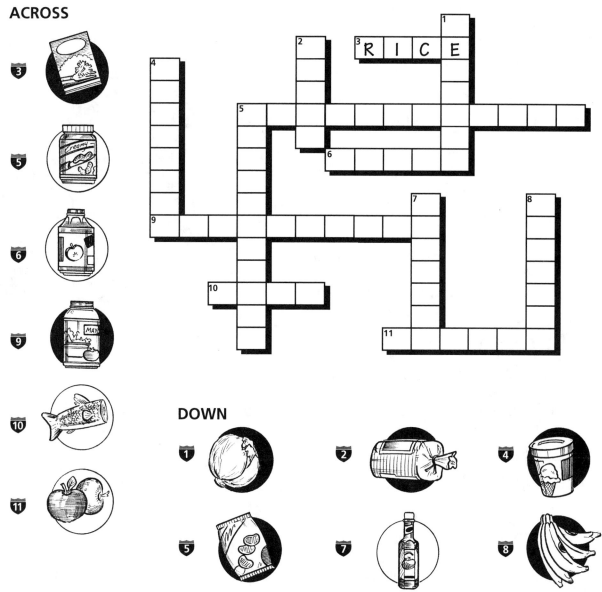

DOWN

D. What's the Word?

Complete the food items.

head	box	loaf	quart	dozen	can	jar	bag

1. a _____box_____ of cookies
2. a _____ of bread
3. a _____ of tuna fish
4. a _____ of lettuce

5. a _____ eggs
6. a _____ of orange juice
7. a _____ of potato chips
8. a _____ of mayonnaise

A. Wrong Way!

Put the lines in the correct order.

___ All right. That's a dozen hot dogs and two jars of mustard. Is that it?

_1_ May I help you?

___ Anything else?

___ Yes. That's it.

___ Yes. I also want two jars of mustard.

___ Yes, please. I want a dozen hot dogs.

B. Listen

Listen and circle the food item you hear.

1 (a.) a jar of mustard
   b. three jars of mustard

6 a. a pound of potato salad
   b. one pound of potato salad

2 a. a pound of roast beef
   b. a pound of ground beef

7 a. three bottles of mayonnaise
   b. three jars of mayonnaise

3 a. a pint of chocolate ice cream
   b. a pound of chocolate ice cream

8 a. a bag of grapes
   b. a bunch of grapes

4 a. two loaf of white bread
   b. two loaves of white bread

9 a. four pounds of chicken
   b. four pieces of chicken

5 a. half a pound of Swiss cheese
   b. a pound of Swiss cheese

10 a. two dozen rolls
   b. a dozen rolls

C. Matching Lines

Match the lines.

_c_ **1** I want a pound of ____.

___ **2** I'd like a dozen ____.

___ **3** I want six pieces of ____.

___ **4** A loaf of ____, please.

a. rolls

b. white bread

c. ground beef

d. fried chicken

D. Enough or Not Enough?

Are these people going to buy "enough food" or "not enough food" for their guests?

		Enough	*Not Enough*
1	"My sister is coming over for dinner. I'll need to buy two or three lamb chops."	✓	
2	"I'm going to have a party this weekend. I'll need to buy a hot dog and a loaf of bread."		
3	"My brother is coming over for lunch today. I'll need to buy half a pound of roast beef, some mustard, and two or three rolls."		
4	"My daughter's second-grade class is coming to our house for a party. I'll need to buy two or three donuts and a quart of milk."		

E. WordRap: *May I Help You?*

Listen. Then clap and practice.

A. May I help you?

B. Yes, please.
   I'd like a dozen hot dogs,
   A can of peas,
   A jar of mustard,
   And a pound of cheese,
   Two pounds of beef,
   And a box of rice.
   We're having a picnic.

A. Oh, that's nice!

A. Anything else?

B. Let me see.
   I'd like two large jars
   Of strawberry jam,
   A loaf of bread,
   And a pound of ham,
   Two heads of lettuce
   And some onions, too.
   Do you deliver?

A. Of course, we do!

F. Open Road!

You're going to have a picnic with some friends this weekend. Make a shopping list.

A. Wrong Way!

Put the lines in the correct order.

____ All right. Your change is sixteen dollars and forty-two cents.

____ Yes.

____ Thank you.

_1_ That'll be three fifty-eight.

____ Have a nice day.

____ Here's twenty.

____ Three fifty-eight?

B. Matching Lines

Match the lines.

_e_ **1** forty-eight cents

____ **2** thirty dollars and twenty-six cents

____ **3** one ninety-nine

____ **4** eight dollars and five cents

____ **5** thirteen dollars and twenty-six cents

a. $13.26

b. $1.99

c. $30.26

d. $8.05

e. $ .48

C. What's the Change?

What change will you receive?

1 A. That'll be $6.47 with tax.
B. Here's ten.
A. Your change is _____

_____.

2 A. That comes to $56.98.
B. Here's a hundred.
A. Okay. Your change is _____

_____.

D. Listen

Listen and decide if the prices are "likely" or "unlikely."

1 likely   (unlikely)   **3** likely   unlikely   **5** likely   unlikely

2 likely   unlikely   **4** likely   unlikely   **6** likely   unlikely

28

Order Food in a Fast-Food Restaurant

A. The Right Choice

Circle the correct word.

A. Welcome to Carolina Fried Chicken. May I help you?

B. I'd like two [cups / **(pieces)**]¹ of chicken and an [container / order]² of french fries.

A. Do you want anything to drink with that?

B. Yes. I'll have a [cup / order]³ of coffee.

A. Okay. Is that for here or to [eat / go]⁴ ?

B. For [here / her]⁵ .

A. That comes to four dollars and twenty-three cents, please.

B. Here you are.

A. And here's your [order / change]⁶ . Your food will be ready in a moment.

B. Listen

Listen and circle the correct answer.

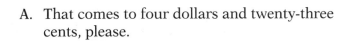

❶	**(fries)**	shake	❹ sandwich	soda
❷	tacos	coffee	❺ iced tea	chicken
❸	small salad	hamburgers	❻ cheeseburger	cole slaw

29

C. Listen

Listen to the order and choose the correct item.

1 —— two large orders of french fries
✔ a large order of french fries

2 —— a cup of cole slaw
—— a cup of coffee

3 —— twelve tacos
—— two tacos

4 —— three pieces of chicken
—— three large chickens

5 —— an order of french fries
—— an order of refried beans

6 —— a chocolate shake
—— a chocolate soda

7 —— a ground beef sandwich
—— a roast beef sandwich

8 —— two fish salads
—— two fish sandwiches

9 —— a medium Coke
—— a small Coke

10 —— three cheeseburgers
—— three hamburgers

D. Mix-Up!

The orders are all mixed up! Put the words in the correct order.

I'd like a cup of fries and an order of coffee.

I'd like an order of fries and
a cup of coffee.

1

Ten pieces of soda and a small orange chicken, please.

2

I'd like a vanilla sandwich and a fish shake.

4

I'll have a roast beef iced tea and a medium sandwich.

3

I'd like a container of lemonade and a medium cole slaw.

5

A. What's the Response?

Choose the correct response.

1. What would you like?
   a. I like fish.
   b. I'd like the fish. *(circled)*

2. Would you prefer noodles or rice?
   a. I'd prefer noodles.
   b. I prefer noodles.

3. Would you like anything to drink?
   a. Yes. I'd like a glass of mineral water.
   b. No. I'd like a glass of mineral water.

B. Wrong Way!

Put the lines in the correct order.

_7_ Two more glasses? Of course.

_6_ Yes. Could we please have two more glasses of iced tea?

_4_ Could you also take back this potato? It isn't cooked.

_1_ Is everything all right with your meal?

_2_ Well, actually this roast beef is cold.

_5_ I see. Anything else?

_3_ I'm terribly sorry. I'll take it back to the kitchen.

C. Food Match

Match the words and the food items.

noodles	meat loaf	rice	spaghetti
mashed potatoes	baked beans	fish	lamb chops

1. _fish_   2. _____   3. _____   4. _____

5. _____   6. _____   7. _____   8. _____

D. Listen

Listen and circle the correct answer.

1	coffee	(milk)		**4**	rice	tea
2	potatoes	fries		**5**	beans	potato
3	loaf	chops		**6**	Pepsi	noodles

E. Scrambled Foods

Unscramble the following foods.

1 t t a o o p _____potato_____   **4** k i e c c n h _____

2 s o n d e l o _____   **5** m b a l s o h c p _____

3 h i a e t s t g p _____   **6** d e b k a a n s e b _____

F. The 5th Wheel!

Which one doesn't belong?

1	coffee	(beans)	tea	water
2	iced	rice	noodles	beans
3	lamb chops	fish	chicken	roast beef
4	want	help	like	prefer

G. Open Road!

You're ordering dinner at a restaurant. Order anything you'd like.

A. May I help you?

B. Yes. I'll have ....

A. And what would you like with that?

B. Let me see. I'd like ....

A. And would you like anything to drink?

B. Hmm. I think I'll have ....

A. Okay. That's ....

with .... and a

....

A. The Right Choice

Circle the correct word.

A. Would you like a little / few¹ more mushrooms?

B. It's / They're² excellent . . . but no, thank you.

A. Oh, come on! Have a few / little³ more.

B. All right. But please . . . not too much / many⁴.

A. Would you like a little / few⁵ more pie?

B. They're / It's⁶ very good . . . but no, thank you.

A. Oh, come on! Have a few / little⁷ more.

B. All right. But please . . . not too much / many⁸ .

B. Listen

Listen and circle the correct answer.

1. meatballs   (ice cream)   3. meat loaf   baked potatoes
2. cookies   salad   4. noodles   rice

33

C. What's the Word?

Complete the following.

few	little	many	much

Bob likes to go to his friend Sally's house for dinner. Sally is a very good cook. How ___much___ [1] food does Bob eat at Sally's house? He always eats too _____ [2]! Sally makes a very good salad. Bob tries to eat only a _____ [3], but he usually eats too _____ [4]. Sally also makes fantastic meatballs! Bob always eats too _____ [5]. When Sally offers him more meatballs, he always eats a _____ [6] more. For dessert, there are usually cookies and ice cream. Bob thinks that Sally's cookies are wonderful! How _____ [7] cookies does he eat? Too _____ [8]! And how _____ [9] ice cream does he eat? You guessed it! He always eats too _____ [10]!

D. Matching Lines

Match the lines.

_c_ **1** How ____ tacos do you want?

____ **2** How ____ salad is left?

____ **3** May I have a ____ more egg rolls?

____ **4** I'd like a ____ more bread and cheese.

a. much

b. little

c. many

d. few

E. Open Road!

Roger made a New Year's resolution this year. He says he isn't going to eat too many cookies or too much ice cream! How about you? Do you have any resolutions?

Next year ....

....

....

Give and Follow Recipe Instructions

A. The Right Choice

Circle the correct word.

A. Your stew is delicious. Can you tell me the recipe?

B. Sure. First, (add (mix))[1] together meatballs, onions, mushrooms, and carrots.

A. I see.

B. Then, (add   put)[2] salt and (add   put)[3] the mixture in a pan. Are you with me so far?

A. Yes. I'm following you.

B. Okay. Next, (bake   serve)[4] it in the oven for one and a half hours at 375 degrees.

A. Uh-húh.

B. And then, (bake   serve)[5] it with bread and a salad. Have you got all that?

A. Yes, I've got it. Thanks.

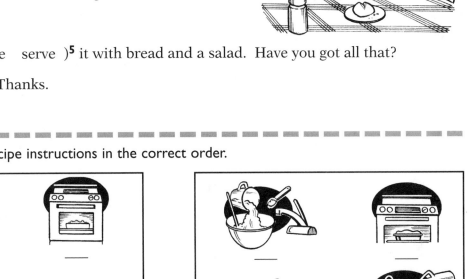

B. Listen

Listen and put the recipe instructions in the correct order.

_____   _____

_____ 1 _____

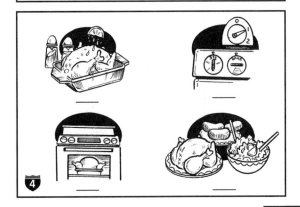

C. Matching Lines

Match the lines.

<u> c </u> **1** Can you tell me the recipe?

____ **2** Tell me, are the chocolate chip cookies easy to make?

____ **3** Do you like to eat at McDon's fast food restaurant?

____ **4** How many do you want?

____ **5** How much cake do you want?

____ **6** Are supermarkets convenient?

____ **7** Did you say seventeen dollars? Here's twenty.

____ **8** Is that for here or to go?

a. I'd like just a little, please.

b. Yes. I love the hamburgers and the french fries there.

c. Sure. First, mix together some butter and sugar.

d. And your change is three dollars.

e. Not too many. Just a few.

f. It's for here.

g. Yes. You can shop for food in just one place and save time.

h. Yes, they are. The recipe is very easy.

D. What's the Word?

Complete the food items.

water	slaw	loaf	chicken	fries	dogs
chops	beans	tea	beef	chips	cream

1 fried <u>chicken</u>

2 lamb _____

3 roast _____

4 meat _____

5 french _____

6 refried _____

7 mineral _____

8 iced _____

9 cole _____

10 hot _____

11 potato _____

12 ice _____

E. Open Road!

Give instructions for your favorite recipe.

◆◆◆◆   ◆◆◆◆   ◆◆◆◆   ◆◆◆◆   ◆◆◆◆

My recipe for ....

First, ...

Then, ...

Next, ...

And then, ...

A. The Right Choice

Circle the correct word.

1 When / (Where) are you from?

5 When / What are you doing?

2 Why / Which are you here?

6 Who / What do you call collect?

3 When / Who did you call them?

7 Why / When is the next train to Chicago?

4 Which / Who floor do you live on?

8 What / Who do you order at that restaurant?

B. What's the Word?

Complete the sentences.

me	him	her	us	you	them

1 Here's my address. Please write ___me___ a letter.

2 It's my sister's birthday tomorrow. I'm going to send _____ flowers.

3 My new neighbors are very nice. I want you to meet _____.

4 We're going to plant a garden. Do you want to help _____?

5 Richard can't find his wallet. Can you lend _____ some money?

6 I'll be glad to help _____ do your English homework.

7 I'm making chocolate chip cookies. Can you give _____ a few eggs?

C. The Right Choice

Circle the correct word.

1 Put [off / (away)] the dishes.

2 Take [up / out] the garbage.

3 Pick [away / up] the mess.

4 Get [up / off] the train.

5 Cut [down / out] those trees.

6 Put [off / away] the books.

7 Mix [together / from] the ingredients.

8 Clean [up / down] the kitchen.

D. Listen

Listen and circle the word you hear.

1 buy   (bought)   **4** sat   sit   **7** get   got

2 spent   spend   **5** ride   rode   **8** wake up   woke up

3 take   took   **6** had   have   **9** eat   ate

E. The Right Choice

Circle the correct word.

1 ((Is) Does) there a bus stop nearby?

2 We need a (pound quart) of milk.

3 I (wasn't didn't) hear you.

4 (Am Can) I leave my bike here?

5 I'd like a (bunch head) of bananas.

6 How (much many) eggs do we have?

7 He (won't don't) be here until Friday.

8 (Was Did) you hear something?

9 The stove (isn't doesn't) working.

10 (Do Will) he be back soon?

11 Have a (little few) more salad.

12 (Do May) I speak to Mr. Jansen?

13 (Could Would) I please have a cup of tea?

14 What are you (do doing)?

Evaluate the Affordability of Items in a Store

**Student Text
Pages 66–69**

A. The Right Choice

Circle the correct answer.

A. Which chair do you like?

B. I like this one. It's very ((nice) nicer)[1].

A. I know. It's (nice   nicer)[2] than that one,
but it's also (expensive   more expensive)[3].

B. Hmm. You're right.

A. I don't think we can afford it.

B. I suppose not.

B. More Right Choices

Circle the correct answer.

1 This small fan is more powerful than that large one. Let's buy the
((small) large) one.

2 The blue chair is more comfortable than the yellow one. I think
we should buy the (blue   yellow) one.

3 Let's buy this air conditioner. It's (noisier   quieter) than that one.

4 I like this rug very much. It's much (uglier   prettier) than that one.

5 I think that crib is much (more powerful   nicer) than this one.

6 This dishwasher is (more expensive   cheaper) than that one.
I don't think we can afford it.

7 I like this CD player. It's much (more comfortable   better)
than that one.

8 These brown shoes are much more attractive than those black shoes over there.
I think you should buy the (brown   black) shoes.

9 Of course we can afford this computer. It's (more expensive   cheaper) than the
computer at the other store.

10 This shirt is too large. You need to buy a (larger   smaller) one.

11 Mommy, I like this doll better than that doll. It's (prettier   uglier) than that one.
And you'll be happy because it's also (more expensive   cheaper).

C. Matching Lines

Match the lines.

_a_ **1** This washing machine isn't very quiet.

____ **2** This sofa is nicer than that one.

____ **3** These gloves are more comfortable than those gloves.

____ **4** Those shirts are cheaper than these shirts.

____ **5** This rug isn't very attractive.

____ **6** This CD player is better than that one.

a. You're right. Let's buy that one.

b. I agree. Let's buy this one.

c. That's true. I think we should buy those.

d. I agree. I think we should buy these.

e. I agree. We should buy it.

f. I know. We shouldn't buy it.

D. Crosswalk

ACROSS

2 Those gloves are very large. Try these gloves. They're _____ than those.

5 A color TV is more expensive than a black-and-white TV. A black-and-white TV is _____ .

6 That doll is ugly! We need to find a _____ one.

7 This air conditioner is very noisy! I need to buy a _____ one.

DOWN

1 This rug isn't very attractive. That one is _____ .

3 That computer isn't very powerful. I think this one is _____ .

4 This crib isn't very good. I need to buy a _____ one.

40

A. Wrong Way!

Put the lines in the correct order.

____ Take a look at this one. It's the most dependable dryer in the store.

____ Three hundred and seventy-five dollars.

_1_ May I help you?

____ Of course. I'll be happy to.

____ I see. Can you show me a less expensive one?

____ Yes. I'm looking for a dependable dryer.

____ How much is it?

B. Description Match

Write the correct description under each picture.

the firmest	the most talkative	the most comfortable
the most nutritious	the most dangerous	the most powerful
the most expensive	the quietest	the most lightweight

1 <u>the most lightweight</u>

2 _____

3 _____

4 _____

5 _____

6 _____

7 _____

8 _____

9 _____

41

C. Listen

Listen to the advertisements and check the words you hear.

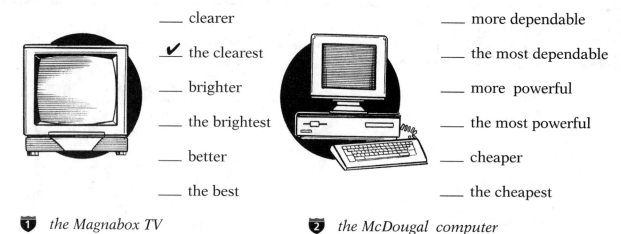

___ clearer

✔ the clearest

___ brighter

___ the brightest

___ better

___ the best

1 *the Magnabox TV*

___ more dependable

___ the most dependable

___ more powerful

___ the most powerful

___ cheaper

___ the cheapest

2 *the McDougal computer*

D. The Right Choice

Circle the correct answer.

1 This is the (firmer (firmest)) mattress in the store.

2 I like this bookcase. It's (larger   largest) than that one over there.

3 I'm looking for a (best   good) cassette player.

4 Is this the (big   biggest) table you have?

5 This is very expensive. Can you show me a (cheaper   more expensive) one?

6 I'm looking for the (more lightweight   most lightweight) sweater you have.

7 Can you please show me a less (expensive   cheaper) one?

8 These gloves are (the most comfortable   more comfortable) than those.

E. Sense or Nonsense?

Do the following "make sense" or are they "nonsense"?

	Sense	*Nonsense*
1 "Don't buy these shoes. They're comfortable."	___	✔
2 "This is a powerful computer. We should buy it."	___	___
3 "Let's buy this sofa. It isn't very attractive."	___	___
4 "Let's buy this stereo. It's the best one they have."	___	___
5 "I don't like talkative parrots. Let's buy this one. It's very quiet."	___	___
6 "I think we should buy this dryer. It's less dependable than that one."	___	___

Budget Your Money

A. The Right Choice

Circle the correct word. Then decide on the amount of money.

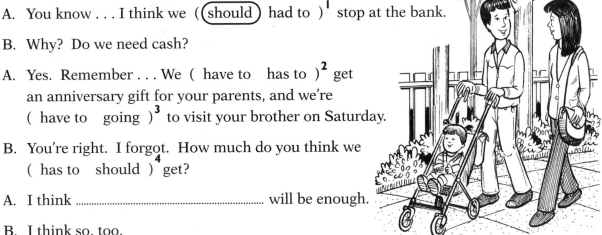

A. You know . . . I think we ((should) had to)¹ stop at the bank.

B. Why? Do we need cash?

A. Yes. Remember . . . We (have to   has to)² get an anniversary gift for your parents, and we're (have to   going)³ to visit your brother on Saturday.

B. You're right. I forgot. How much do you think we (has to   should)⁴ get?

A. I think .... will be enough.

B. I think so, too.

B. Matching Lines

Match the lines.

_d_ **1** We're going skiing tomorrow.

____ **2** Rita doesn't have any gas in her car.

____ **3** We should stop at the bank.

____ **4** How much do you think we should get?

____ **5** I have a big English exam this Friday.

a. You're right. We need cash.

b. Do you have to study all week?

c. She has to buy some.

d. Do you have to rent skis?

e. Fifty dollars will be enough.

C. WordRap: *Money Problems!*

Listen. Then clap and practice.

A. Maybe we should get some money, honey.
Maybe we should cash a check.

B. Maybe we should go to the bank, Frank.
Our weekly budget is a wreck!

A. Our weekly budget is a wreck?!

B. Yes! Our weekly budget is a wreck!

A. I need some change for the phone, Joan.
We need some money for the rent.

B. But we can't get cash from the cash machine.
'Cause all of our money is spent!

A. All of our money is spent?!

B. Yes! All of our money is spent!

A. What's the Response?

Choose the correct response.

1 I'd like to deposit this in my savings account.
   a. Please print your name on the deposit slip.
   b. Please cash this check.

2 I'd like to cash this check.
   a. Yes, you do.
   b. Please write your account number on the back.

3 Did I forget to sign the check?
   a. Yes, you did.
   b. Yes, you do.

5 I need to cash my paycheck.
   a. Please endorse it.
   b. Please sign the withdrawal slip.

4 I'd like to make a withdrawal.
   a. Please sign your name on the deposit slip.
   b. Please sign your name on the withdrawal slip.

6 I'd like to deposit this in my account.
   a. Put your address on the deposit slip, please.
   b. Put your money on the deposit slip, please.

B. Open Road!

Follow the instructions.

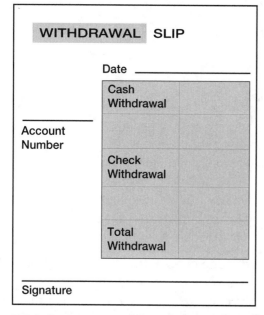

Withdraw money from your account. Make a cash withdrawal and a check withdrawal.

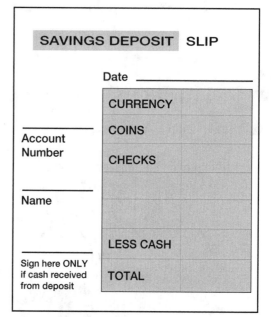

Deposit a check in your account. Get some cash back.

A. Wrong Way!

Put the lines in the correct order.

____ Oh. I forgot to tell you. I wrote a check to Barry's Clothing for a skirt and a sweater.

____ Okay. Thanks.

_1_ What are you doing?

____ Yes. Sixty-six dollars.

____ I'm balancing the checkbook.

____ Oh. Do you remember the amount?

B. Listen

Listen and circle the word you hear.

1	(textbooks)	tests		6	CDs	TVs
2	textbook	checkbook		7	credit card bill	checking account bill
3	$25.00	$125.00		8	$152.60	$162.50
4	amount	account		9	vitamins	medicine
5	$30.00	$13.00		10	sign	endorse

C. Open Road!

You just bought something special. Now you have to pay for it. Write a check.

PAY TO THE
ORDER OF _____ $ _____

_____ Dollars

FOR _____

2:364967:0055

Understand Denominations of Money

A. Coin Match

Match the coin with its name.

penny — 1 cent	nickel — 5 cents	dime — 10 cents	quarter — 25 cents

1 quarter
25 cents

2 _____
_____

3 _____
_____

4 _____
_____

B. What's the Word?

penny — pennies	nickel — nickels	dime — dimes	quarter — quarters

1
A. I'm going to get some soda. Do you want anything?

B. Sure. Please get me a soda, too. That's sixty-five cents, right?

A. Yes, sixty-five cents.

B. Okay. Here's two quarters, a dime, and a _____nickel_____ .

2
A. I'm going to get some ice cream. Do you want anything?

B. Sure. Please get me a cup of vanilla ice cream. That's eighty cents, right?

A. Yes, eighty cents.

B. Okay. Here's a nickel and three _____.

3
A. I'm trying to buy a cup of coffee, but I just lost my money!

B. What did you put in?

A. A quarter, two nickels, and a _____.

B. Forty-five cents? That's too bad!

4
A. I'm trying to buy some gum, but I just lost my money!

B. What did you put in?

A. Nine _____.

B. Nine cents! That's too bad!

Evaluate Payment of Household Bills

A. What's the Date?

Complete each sentence with the correct date.

1. Tom and Jane Ross have to pay the telephone bill on ___September second___.

2. The cable TV bill isn't due yet. It's due on _____.

3. They have to pay the gas bill soon. It's due on _____.

4. Jane is sure the water bill is due on _____.

5. They have to pay the oil bill on _____.

6. The electric bill is due on _____.

B. Matching Lines

Match the months with their abbreviations.

_f_ 1 June   a. APR

___ 2 December   b. JUL

___ 3 May   c. AUG

___ 4 February   d. OCT

___ 5 August   e. MAR

___ 6 January   f. JUN

___ 7 November   g. SEPT

___ 8 March   h. FEB

___ 9 September   i. DEC

___ 10 April   j. NOV

___ 11 October   k. JAN

___ 12 July   l. MAY

C. Listen

Marcia is very busy this month. There are a lot of dates in June she has to remember. Listen and write the number of each special occasion on Marcia's calendar.

JUNE						
Sunday	Monday	Tuesday	Wednesday	Thursday	Friday	Saturday
___ 1	___ 2	___ 3	___ 4	___ 1 5	___ 6	___ 7
___ 8	___ 9	___ 10	___ 11	___ 12	___ 13	___ 14
___ 15	___ 16	___ 17	___ 18	___ 19	___ 20	___ 21
___ 22	___ 23	___ 24	___ 25	___ 26	___ 27	___ 28
___ 29	___ 30					

D. Wrong Way!

Unscramble the words.

1 h f i f t   _____fifth_____   4 w n i t t e t h e _____

2 o s d n e c   _____   5 r o h f u t   _____

3 h r i t t i t e h _____   6 t d i h r   _____

E. Open Road!

Complete the following.

1 What's your favorite day of the year? ....

   Why? ....

2 In your opinion, what's the most exciting day of the year? ....

   Why? ....

A. Wrong Way!

Put the lines in the correct order.

____ All right, Ms. Rodriguez. Please hold, and I'll check our records.

____ I believe I was charged too much.

____ Finally, what is the amount on your bill?

____ Thank you.

_1_ Vision Cable Company. May I help you?

____ And what is your account number, Ms. Rodriguez?

____ Seventy-six dollars and fifteen cents ($76.15).

____ Oh. What's the problem?

____ Carmen Rodriguez.

____ 677-4533-9812-003.

____ I see. I need some information. First, what is your name?

____ Yes. I think there's a mistake on my cable TV bill.

B. The 5th Wheel!

Which one doesn't belong?

1 (dollar bill)	penny	nickel	quarter
2 car payment	electric bill	paycheck	mortgage payment
3 checkbook	kitchen table	account number	check register
4 budget	expenses	savings	apples
5 oil bill	make a deposit	make a withdrawal	cash a check
6 crib	cassette player	computer	stereo system
7 JAN	SAT	OCT	JUL
8 first	three	fourth	fifth
9 nicer	better	best	more powerful

C. Listen

Listen to the conversations and choose the correct answer.

1. **a.** The amount isn't correct.
   b. The account isn't correct.

2. a. The gas bill is for $30.00.
   b. The gas bill is for $300.00.

3. a. This person checked the account balance with a calculator.
   b. This person balanced the calculator.

4. a. This person writes down what she spends each month.
   b. This person doesn't write down her monthly expenses.

5. a. This person adds a lot to his savings account every month.
   b. This person knows how much he can add to his savings account every month.

6. a. This person's telephone bill is due on the 20th.
   b. This person will get a telephone on the 20th.

7. a. This person has to cash a check.
   b. This person has to write a check.

8. a. There's a mistake on the tuition bill.
   b. This person asks the amount of a tuition bill.

D. A Good Idea or Not a Good Idea?

Decide if each of these is a good idea or is not a good idea.

		A Good Idea	Not a Good Idea
1	"Balance your checkbook every month!"	✓	
2	"Buy a car you can't afford!"		
3	"Buy products on sale!"		
4	"Stop at a bank to get cash!"		
5	"Buy gloves that aren't comfortable!"		
6	"Spend all your money every week!"		
7	"Save some money every month!"		
8	"Enter information about every check in your check register!"		
9	"First, decide on a product you want to buy. Second, compare prices at two different stores. Third, buy the product at the most expensive price."		

A. What's the Word?

Complete the conversations.

her	him	them

1. Please fax this report to the company directors.

Certainly. I'll ___fax them___ the report this afternoon.

2. Will you give this package to Mr. Lee on the first floor?

Sure. I'll _____ the package right away.

3. Please mail this letter to my daughter.

Certainly. I'll _____ the letter right now.

4. Can you read a story to the children?

Of course. I'll _____ a story right now.

5. Please send an e-mail to the customers.

Certainly. I'll _____ an e-mail right away.

6. Will you please write a thank-you note to your grandmother?

Okay. I'll _____ a thank-you note this afternoon.

B. Matching Lines

Which of these go together?

_d_	**1** fax machine	a.	numbers
___	**2** computer	b.	news
___	**3** telephone	c.	e-mail
___	**4** Shipping Department	d.	fax a memo
___	**5** announcement	e.	packages

A. What's the Line?

Complete the conversations.

1
Do you want me to clean up the office?

No. That's okay. I can ___clean it up___ later.

2
Would you like me to set up the conference room?

Yes. Please _____ right now.

3
Would you like me to hang up these signs?

Thanks. Can you _____ _____ today?

4
Do you want me to give out these memos?

Good idea! Please _____ _____ now.

5
Do you want me to put away the dishes?

No, that's okay. I can _____ _____ later.

6
I'll be happy to take down the decorations.

Thanks. Please _____ _____ anytime.

B. Listen

Listen and circle the correct answer.

1 (take them down)   take him down

2 call them   call him

3 put them away   put him away

4 clean it up   clean them up

5 give him   give them

6 hang them up   hang up

52

C. The 5th Wheel!

Which one doesn't belong?

1 memo	note	letter	(telephone)
2 package	computer	fax machine	telephone
3 factory	office	mechanic's garage	computer
4 give out	up	put away	clean up
5 over there	right now	anytime today	right away
6 conference room	supply room	mail room	reports
7 customer	announcement	Mr. Jones	Ms. Sanchez

D. Open Road!

Write your own sentences.

take down	set up	put away	hang up	give out	clean up

1 ....
....

2 ....
....

3 ....
....

4 ....
....

5 ....
....

6 ....
....

Give Feedback at Work

A. The Right Choice

Circle the correct word.

1 You paint very (careful (carefully))!

2 You're a very (fast   faster) assembler!

3 You're a very (neatly   neat) worker!

4 Mrs. Wong teaches very (well   good)!

5 You dance very (gracefully   graceful)!

6 You're a very (accurately   accurate) worker!

B. Analogies

| teaches | acts | accurate | positive feedback |
| well | waiter | dancer | computer |

1 dancer : dances *as* teacher : _____ *teaches* _____

2 translator : translates *as* actor : _____

3 accurate : translator *as* graceful : _____

4 carefully : careful *as* accurately : _____

5 neat : neatly *as* good : _____

6 fax : fax machine *as* e-mail : _____

7 assemble : assembler *as* waits on tables : _____

8 "That's bad!" : negative feedback *as* "That's good!" : _____

C. Listen

Who am I? Listen and circle the correct answer.

1 (dancer)   typist

2 assembler   teacher

3 translator   actor

4 waiter   typist

5 assembler   dancer

6 teacher   painter

7 translator   waiter

8 teacher   mechanic

9 actor   assembler

10 translator   interviewer

11 student   teacher

12 typist   police officer

54

D. Open Road!

How do you do the following things?

| accurately | gracefully | neatly | carefully | well | fast |

I sing very well.

I don't dance very gracefully.

I work very neatly.

1. I sing ....
2. I dance ....
3. I act ....
4. I work ....
5. I translate ....
6. I speak English ....
7. I paint ....

8. I type ....
9. I assemble things ....
10. I cook ....
11. I balance my checkbook ....
12. I ....
13. I ....
14. I ....

E. WordRap: *Good Workers*

Listen. Then clap and practice.

He's a very good typist.
He types very well.
He types very quickly.
And he knows how to spell.

She's a wonderful dancer.
She dances very well.
She dances very gracefully.
Can't you tell?

We're very fast assemblers.
We're extremely quick.
Our work is always finished,
Even when we're sick.

They're very good painters.
They have what it takes.
They paint very carefully.
They never make mistakes.

A. What's the Response?

Choose the correct response.

1 Am I working fast enough?
   a. Yes, you are.
   b. No. You should try to work more politely.

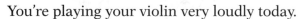

2 You're playing your violin very loudly today.
   a. I'll try to play it louder.
   b. I'll try to play it softer.

3 Am I dancing gracefully enough?
   a. You should try to dance more gracefully.
   b. You should try to dance more neatly.

4 Am I explaining this well enough?
   a. Yes. You're explaining it very well.
   b. Yes. You should explain it better.

5 You should try to speak to your teachers more politely.
   a. Should I speak more politely?
   b. Okay. I'll try to speak more politely.

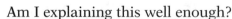

6 You aren't doing this carefully enough.
   a. Thank you.
   b. I'll try to work more carefully.

7 You really should work more quickly.
   a. Okay. I'll try to work a little faster.
   b. Thank you. I'll try to work more slowly.

B. Crosswalk

```
      1
  2 [M][O][R][E][C][A][R][E][F][U][L][L][Y]    3
  4 [ ][ ][ ][ ]                               [ ]
                        5                       [ ]
  6 [ ][ ][ ][ ][ ][ ][ ][ ][ ]                [ ]
                        [ ]                     [ ]
                        [ ]
                        [ ]
```

ACROSS

2 You don't drive very carefully. You should try to drive _____.

4 You're typing too slowly. You should type _____.

6 Some waiters don't speak politely. They should try to speak _____.

DOWN

1 You didn't paint very well last week. Please try to paint _____.

3 You don't usually speak loudly enough. Please try to speak _____.

5 You don't drive your car very slowly. Please try to drive _____.

C. The Right Choice

Circle the correct word.

1 Roland, you aren't playing your guitar loud enough. You ((should) shouldn't) try to play it louder.

2 Arthur (is isn't) a good cashier. He doesn't speak very politely to the customers.

3 Mrs. Anderson (speaks doesn't speak) very slowly. I understand everything she says.

4 Carmen (is isn't) very accurate. She's a very good employee.

5 Richard (is isn't) a very good dancer. He should try to dance more gracefully.

6 Michael (works doesn't work) very slowly. He should try to work faster.

7 Alice (is isn't) a very careful painter. She should try to paint more carefully.

8 You're a very good typist. You (type don't type) very well.

9 Patty is a fast assembler. She works very (quickly slowly).

10 Mrs. Chen is a very accurate translator. She (always never) makes mistakes.

11 Mr. Greenley (is isn't) a very good teacher. He doesn't explain things very well.

Apologize

A. The Right Choice

Circle the correct answer.

1 A. I'm sorry. (I'll be able to (I won't be able to))
        attend your press conference this afternoon.
     B. Oh? Why not?
     A. I (have to   had to) welcome a visitor from
        Brazil.
     B. No problem. It's okay.

2 A. I'm sorry that I (was able to   wasn't able to)
        work late last Friday.
     B. That's all right.
     A. The reason is that I (have to   had to) go to
        the dentist.
     B. I understand. Don't worry about it.

3 A. I'm sorry that I (could   couldn't) finish the
        report yesterday.
     B. That's all right.
     A. The reason is that I (have to   had to) meet
        with my supervisor.
     B. I understand. Don't worry about it.

B. Listen

Yesterday or tomorrow? Listen and circle the correct answer.

1 (yesterday)   tomorrow   **8**   yesterday   tomorrow
2 yesterday   tomorrow   **9**   yesterday   tomorrow
3 yesterday   tomorrow   **10** yesterday   tomorrow
4 yesterday   tomorrow   **11** yesterday   tomorrow
5 yesterday   tomorrow   **12** yesterday   tomorrow
6 yesterday   tomorrow   **13** yesterday   tomorrow
7 yesterday   tomorrow   **14** yesterday   tomorrow

C. What's the Line?

Complete the following excuses.

| will/won't be able to have to | was/wasn't able to has to | were/weren't able to had to | could/couldn't |

1 I'm sorry that I __won't be able to__ come to your party tonight. I ____have to____ work late.

2 I'm happy my husband and I _____ come to your house for dinner next weekend. But we'll _____ leave early to pick up our daughter.

3 Henry _____ come to work early yesterday. He _____ take his car to the mechanic.

4 Mr. President, you _____ attend the press conference this afternoon. You _____ meet with the French ambassador.

5 My children _____ go to school yesterday. They _____ go to the doctor.

6 Dr. Denton _____ see you on Thursday morning because he _____ be at the hospital. But I'm sure the doctor _____ see you on Friday.

7 I'm sorry that I _____ come to the meeting yesterday. I _____ start my car.

D. Matching Lines

Which words go together?

_h_	**1** hang up	a.	forgot
___	**2** have to	b.	bought
___	**3** go	c.	took
___	**4** forget	d.	got
___	**5** get	e.	had to
___	**6** take	f.	said
___	**7** say	g.	went
___	**8** buy	h.	hung up

Report an Emergency

A. What's the Response?

Choose the correct response.

1 Joe burned himself on the stove!
  a. Tell him to press the burn!
  b. Tell him to put cold water on the burn! *(circled)*

2 What happened?
  a. My sister poked herself in the eye!
  b. Let's go to the nurse's office!

3 I hurt myself on the machine!
  a. I'll call the hospital!
  b. I'll call you!

4 You won't believe what happened!
  a. Be careful!
  b. What happened?

5 Those girls spilled tea all over themselves!
  a. I'll get the first-aid kit!
  b. You won't believe what happened!

6 That parrot talks to itself all the time!
  a. I'll call a doctor!
  b. What does it say?

7 Sam and I cut ourselves!
  a. Are you bleeding very badly?
  b. Are they bleeding very badly?

8 Did you hurt yourself?
  a. Yes. Call a first-aid kit!
  b. Yes. Call a doctor!

B. Matching Lines

Match the lines.

_e_ **1** Frank, you cut ___!   a. itself

___ **2** My husband hurt ___!   b. ourselves

___ **3** I shocked ___!   c. themselves

___ **4** My sister poked ___!   d. himself

___ **5** We spilled soup all over ___!   e. yourself

___ **6** Grandma and Grandpa talk to ___.   f. herself

___ **7** The cat hurt ___!   g. yourselves

___ **8** I'm sorry that you and your friends cut ___.   h. myself

C. Listen

Listen and circle the word you hear.

1. yourself (yourselves)
2. ourselves   themselves
3. myself   itself

4. himself   herself
5. ourselves   yourselves
6. herself   itself

7. himself   herself
8. yourselves   yourself
9. themselves   himself

D. The Right Choice

Circle the correct word,

The Lin family had very bad luck yesterday. Mr. Lin went to work and had to stay late to help take inventory. Mr. Lin took a box down from a shelf, and the box hit him on the head. He hurt (herself (himself))[1], and he had to go to the doctor. He couldn't go to work today.

Mrs. Lin works in a factory. Yesterday her supervisor said to her, "Please work faster." Mrs. Lin tried to work faster, but she hurt (himself   herself)[2] on her machine. They had to turn off all the power in the factory, and Mrs. Lin had to go to the hospital. She won't be able to go to work today.

Yesterday Grandma and Grandpa Lin walked to the supermarket. A car hit them and they hurt (yourselves   themselves)[3]. They had to get first-aid. Grandma and Grandpa Lin have to stay home today.

Timmy and Peter Lin went to school yesterday. They went to Biology class. The teacher said, "Be careful! Don't cut (ourselves   yourselves)[4]!" But Timmy and Peter weren't very careful and they cut (themselves   ourselves)[5]. They'll be able to go to school again tomorrow.

At 6:00 P.M. Sally decided to help with dinner. But she burned (himself   herself)[6] on the stove and spilled hot water on the dog. The dog burned (myself   itself)[7] very badly and had to go to the animal hospital.

Everyone in the Lin family is at home today. They all had very bad luck yesterday!

61

A. Wrong Way!

Put the lines in the correct order.

____ Hmm. Well, I'm not really sure.

____ Well, in that case, of course you can leave an hour early.

_1_ Excuse me, Mr. Butler.

____ Could I possibly leave an hour early?

____ Thank you very much.

____ Yes?

____ The reason I'm asking is my daughter burned herself and I have to take her to the doctor.

B. A Good Excuse or Not a Good Excuse?

Decide if each of the following is "a good excuse" or is "not a good excuse."

		A Good Excuse	Not a Good Excuse
1	"I'm sorry I can't come to the meeting this afternoon. I have to go to the doctor."	✓	_____
2	"I won't be able to help take inventory tomorrow because I have to see a movie."	_____	_____
3	"Could I possibly leave a half hour early? My son hurt himself at school."	_____	_____
4	"I'm sorry I won't be able to finish the report. I have to buy some food at the supermarket."	_____	_____
5	"Could I possibly take the day off tomorrow? My parrot is sick."	_____	_____
6	"I'm really sorry I wasn't able to come in early today. My car didn't start and I had to take the bus."	_____	_____
7	"I'm sorry I wasn't able to stay until the end of the meeting. I had to get home to watch the football game on TV."	_____	_____

What are these people thinking? Check the most likely answer.

1  *I'll finish all the work before I go home.*

 *I'm impressed.* ✔   *I'm not impressed.*

2  *I can't finish my work because I have to play golf at 5:00.*

 *I'm pleased to hear that.*   *I'm not pleased to hear that.*

3  *Do you think we should set up the conference room now?*

 *This employee has initiative.*   *This employee doesn't have initiative.*

4  *I won't be able to come to work on time tomorrow. I have to clean my house.*

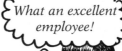 *What an excellent employee!*   *I'm not very pleased to hear that.*

5  *I need to leave work early today. My mother is in the hospital.*

 That's okay.   *That's not okay.*

6  *Your presentation was excellent!*

 *My supervisor complimented me!*   *My supervisor wasn't very pleased.*

Exit 6

Tell What People Aren't Allowed to Do

Student Text Pages 106–109

A. Matching Lines

Match the conversations and the scenes.

   a.

   b.

   c.

   d.

   e.

f.

   g.

   h.

__h__ **1** A. Are you allowed to swim here?
          B. No, you aren't.

___ **2** A. Are you allowed to camp here?
          B. Yes, you are.

___ **3** A. Are you allowed to play ball here?
          B. Yes, you are.

___ **4** A. Are you allowed to ice skate here?
          B. No, aren't.

___ **5** A. Are you allowed to park here?
          B. Yes, you are.

___ **6** A. Are you allowed to eat here?
          B. No, you aren't.

___ **7** A. Are you allowed to walk on the grass?
          B. Yes, you are.

___ **8** A. Are you allowed to come in here?
          B. No, you aren't.

B. Listen

Are you allowed to . . . ? Listen and choose "Yes" or "No."

1 Yes (No)
2 Yes No
3 Yes No

4 No No
5 No No
6 Yes No

7 Yes No
8 Yes No
9 Yes No

C. Same or Different?

Are the meanings of the sentences the same or are they different?

		Same	Different
1	a. "You can't eat in the classroom." b. "You're allowed to eat in the classroom."	_____	✓
2	a. "Keep off the grass." b. "Don't walk on the grass."	_____	_____
3	a. "You aren't supposed to swim in the lake." b. "Swimming is allowed in the lake."	_____	_____
4	a. "You have to move your car." b. "There's no parking here."	_____	_____
5	a. "You can't ice skate here." b. "Ice skating is allowed."	_____	_____
6	a. "You can leave work early today." b. "You aren't allowed to leave work early today."	_____	_____
7	a. "Don't go into the meeting room." b. "You aren't allowed to enter the meeting room."	_____	_____
8	a. "Parking here is for handicapped only." b. "Handicapped people aren't allowed to park here."	_____	_____

D. Open Road!

What are you allowed to do in your English class?

Yes, you are. No, you aren't. Yes, you can. No, you can't.

1 Are you allowed to use dictionaries? ....

2 Are you allowed to speak your native language? ....

3 Are you allowed to eat? ....

4 Can you talk to your friends? ....

5 ....? ....

65

A. What's the Line?

What did the police officer say?

That sign over there.	Yes, that's right.
Do Not Enter!	Didn't you see the sign?

A. What's the matter, Officer?

B. _____Didn't you see the sign?_____ **1**

A. The sign? What sign?

B. _____ **2**

A. What did it say?

B. _____ **3**

A. Do Not Enter?!

B. _____ **4**

A. Oh, my goodness!

B. Fill It In!

Complete the signs.

ONE WAY	NO RIGHT TURN ON RED	NO U TURN
STOP	DO NOT ENTER	NO LEFT TURN

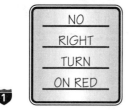

1

2

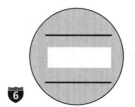

3

4

5

6

A. The Right Choice

Circle the correct word.

A.   Let me see your license.

B.   Here you are, Officer. What [do /(did)]¹ I [do / did]² wrong?

A.   You [are / were]³ going 80 miles per hour.

B.   I [am / was]⁴ going 80 miles per hour?!

A.   Yes. [I'm / I'll]⁵ going to [have to / had to]⁶ give you a ticket.

B.   Oh.

B. Matching Lines

Match the lines.

_g_ ❶ He was driving on the wrong side of the ____.   a. ticket

____ ❷ Don't drive through that red ____!   b. speeding

____ ❸ You were driving 75 miles ____.   c. light

____ ❹ He made an illegal ____.   d. stop sign

____ ❺ She went through a ____.   e. wrong

____ ❻ The officer gave me a ____.   f. per hour

____ ❼ What did I do ____?   g. road

____ ❽ You were ____.   h. left turn

67

C. Listen

Listen and put the number under the traffic violation you hear about.

_____   <u>1</u>   _____

_____   _____

D. What's the Response?

Choose the correct response.

1 What were they doing wrong?
    a. They speeded.
    (b.) They were speeding.

2 What was I doing when you made the wrong turn?
    a. You turned on the radio.
    b. You were listening to the radio.

3 What did Margaret do wrong?
    a. She was going through a red light.
    b. She went through a red light.

4 What were you doing when I called?
    a. I was cooking dinner.
    b. I cooked dinner.

5 What were we doing when the mail came?
    a. We were watching TV.
    b. We talked on the telephone.

6 Why did Gregory get a ticket?
    a. He was going through a red light.
    b. He went through a red light.

E. Open Road!

A police officer stopped you. What did you say to each other?

A. ....

B. ....

A. ....

B. ....

A. ....

B. ....

A. What's the Word?

Complete the conversation.

rules	permitted	know	allowed	Tenants	entrance	building	leave

A. Excuse me, but I don't think you're _____allowed_____ **1** to _____ **2** your car there.

B. Oh?

A. Yes. _____ **3** aren't _____ **4** to leave their cars at the _____ **5**. It's one of the _____ **6** of the _____ **7**.

B. Oh. I didn't _____ **8** that. Sorry.

A. That's okay.

B. What Are the Rules?

New tenants moved into this apartment house on Main Street yesterday. Put a check next to the building rules the new tenants don't know.

RULES OF THE BUILDING

✔ You aren't allowed to cook on the balcony.

✔ Don't put flowerpots on the window ledges.

✔ Don't play your stereo very loudly.

___ You can't leave garbage in the halls.

___ Don't go on the roof.

___ You aren't allowed to hang laundry on the balcony.

___ Tenants aren't permitted to park in front of the entrance.

A. The Right Choice

Circle the correct word.

A. Hello. This is Jane Fergerson in Apartment 303.

B. Yes? What can I do for you?

A. I'm wondering . . . (When) / What [1] are you going to spray our apartment?

B. Well, Ms. Fergerson, I'm very busy right now. I'm / I'll [2] try to spray soon.

A. You promised / promise [3] to spray two weeks ago.

I'll / I'm [4] going to have to call the Health Department.

B. Now, Ms. Fergerson. I'm sure that will / won't [5] be necessary.

I promise I'm / I'll [6] spray today.

A. Thank you very much.

B. Listen

What are they talking about? Listen and circle the correct answer.

1	(the heat)	the Housing Authority		6	the garbage	the superintendent
2	the stereo	the TV station		7	the car	the security deposit
3	the mess	the heat		8	the balcony	the security deposit
4	the toilets	the plumbers		9	the hallway	the bedrooms
5	the hallway	the lead paint		10	the kitchen	the Health Department

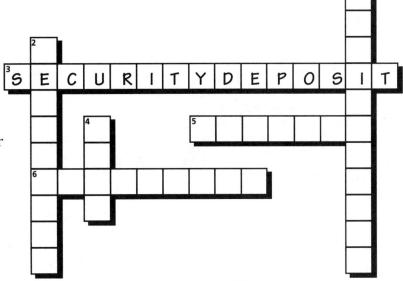

ACROSS

3 I promise I'll return your _____ next week.

5 When are you going to take out the _____?

6 You need to spray our _____.

DOWN

1 I'll fix your stove and your _____ tomorrow.

2 Please remove the _____ from the hallways.

4 I'm going to turn on the _____ today.

D. What's the Response?

Choose the correct response.

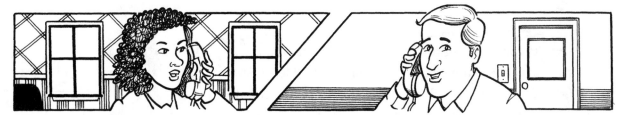

1 I'm upset! I'm going to go to court.
   a. I promise I'll return your security deposit tomorrow.
   b. Am I going with you?

2 I'm afraid I'm going to have to call City Hall.
   a. Please don't make noise after 10 P.M.
   b. I'll fix the heat today.

3 I contacted Channel 6 News yesterday.
   a. That wasn't necessary. I'll remove the lead paint today.
   b. Thank you very much.

4 I promise I'll fix your toilet soon.
   a. You promised to fix it last week.
   b. Toilets aren't permitted in the building.

A. The Right Choice

What are the rules? Circle the correct word.

There are two important rules here at the computer factory. First of all, you (must (mustn't)) go into the restricted area. Also, you (must   mustn't) punch in by 7:30 A.M.

1

Before you begin your new job, I'd like to tell you about two important rules here at the Fried Chicken Shack. First of all, you (must   mustn't) always wear your uniform. Also, you (must   mustn't) chew gum.

2

There are two important rules here at Mike's Repairs. First of all, you (must   mustn't) wear protective glasses. Also, you (must   mustn't) leave the work area without permission.

3

Before you begin your new job, I'd like to tell you about two important rules here at the Flett National Bank. First of all, you (must   mustn't) eat at your desk. Also, you (must   mustn't) greet the customers with a smile.

4

We have some important rules here at the Ajax Corporation. First of all, you (must   musn't) come to work late. Also, you (must   musn't) type all of your work on your computer.

5

72

B. Listen

Listen and choose the correct answer.

1 a. come to work late
   (b.) punch in by 7:45 A.M.

5 a. wear your uniform
   b. ask too many questions

2 a. leave without permission
   b. leave with permission

6 a. work accurately
   b. eat at your workstation

3 a. speak politely to the customers
   b. chew gum at work

7 a. work neatly
   b. make the sundaes too large

4 a. go into the restricted area
   b. wear protective glasses

8 a. be a good employee
   b. forget to follow the rules

C. Open Road!

Officer Petrillo is a new police officer in town. Tell the new officer about some important rules of the job. Check ✔ if he must, or check **x** if he mustn't do the following.

☐ **1** Wear his police uniform.

☐ **2** Give traffic tickets.

☐ **3** Leave work without permission.

☐ **4** Greet people politely.

☐ **5** Drive on the wrong side of the road.

☐ **6** Wear protective glasses.

☐ **7** ....

D. The Right Choice

Circle the correct word.

1 My supervisor says I (can (must)) always come to work on time.

2 I'm not sure about my plans for the weekend. I (must   might) see a movie.

3 My doctor is concerned about my blood pressure. She thinks I (might   should) lose weight.

4 I'm not a good typist. I (can't   might) type very quickly.

5 You (shouldn't   can) do your homework too quickly. You (must   might) make mistakes.

6 We (mustn't   should) go into that restricted area. Employees aren't allowed to go there.

7 I'm not happy at work. I (might   shouldn't) look for a new job.

8 You (must   musn't) follow all the regulations. If you don't follow them, you (might   can't) lose your job.

A. Wrong Way!

Put the lines in the correct order.

_____ The lines at the tollbooths are very long, and people are often late for work.

_____ That's a good idea. I will.

_____ Write to the governor?

_1_ You know . . . in my opinion, they should have more open tollbooths on this road in the morning.

_____ You should write to the governor.

_____ Why do you say that?

_____ Yes. Really. You ought to write to the governor and express your opinion.

B. Open Road!

What should people do? Express your opinion!

PROBLEM	EXPRESS YOUR OPINION
1. The landlord won't fix my heat.	You should call the Housing Authority. You also ought to write to the city manager.
2. The bus is late every morning.	
3. A police officer gave my son a speeding ticket.	
4. The superintendent won't fix our broken steps.	
5. The landlord won't remove the lead paint in the hallway	
6. Our senator isn't doing his job very well.	

C. What's the Meaning?

Choose the sentence that has the same meaning.

1 There ought to be a law.
   a. There is a law.
   (b.) There should be a law.

2 You're allowed to speak at the town meeting.
   a. You ought to speak at the town meeting.
   b. You're permitted to speak at the town meeting.

3 The sign says "Parking for Handicapped Only."
   a. Handicapped people can park here.
   b. Handicapped people can't park here.

4 I contacted the governor
   a. I saw the governor.
   b. I called the governor.

5 Express your opinion.
   a. Say what you think.
   b. Agree with someone.

6 Tenants must have heat during the winter.
   a. It's usually cold outside during the winter.
   b. Landlords have to turn on the heat during the winter.

7 Did you know that you were speeding?
   a. Did you know that you were driving too fast?
   b. Did you know that you were driving too slowly?

8 The mayor apologized to everyone.
   a. The mayor said, "I'm sorry."
   b. The mayor agreed with everyone.

D. Likely or Unlikely?

Are the following statements "likely" or "unlikely"?

		Likely	Unlikely
1	"My doctor says I have to eat rich desserts to lose weight."		✓
2	"We aren't permitted to play loud music after 11 P.M. in our building."		
3	"I wasn't able to come to your party because I had to work."		
4	"My supervisor is impressed because I never come to work on time."		
5	"Our boss says we should type more carefully."		
6	"Students must come late to class."		
7	"The Housing Authority pays my rent."		
8	"Our teacher says we mustn't do our homework."		
9	"You must chew gum at work."		

E. Listen

Listen to the conversations and choose the correct answer.

Conversation 1

1 (a.) This woman called a radio talk show.
  b. This woman called a TV show.

2 a. She wants the city to pick up the garbage every day.
  b. She wants the city to pick up the garbage every week.

3 a. She should write to the Housing Authority.
  b. She should write to the Health Department.

4 a. She should also call the mayor.
  b. She should also call the president.

Conversation 2

5 a. This man is going to write to the president.
  b. This man is going to call the president.

6 a. He thinks cable TV is too cheap.
  b. He thinks cable TV is too expensive.

7 a. He ought to write to the newspaper.
  b. He ought to call a talk radio program.

8 a. Also, he should write to the town meeting.
  b. Also, he should write to his congressman.

F. WordRap: *Somebody Ought To Do Something!*

Listen. Then clap and practice.

Somebody ought to write a letter.
Somebody ought to make a call.
Somebody ought to tell the landlord
There's a terrible smell in the hall!

Somebody ought to write a letter.
Somebody ought to send a fax.
Somebody ought to tell the landlord
The building is full of cracks!

Somebody ought to write a letter.
Somebody ought to make a call.
Somebody ought to tell the landlord
The ceiling's getting ready to fall!

Somebody ought to write a letter.
Somebody ought to send a note.
There's a lot of noise in Apartment 4.
I think they're building a boat!

A. The 5th Wheel!

Which one doesn't belong?

1	(good)	firmest	biggest	best
2	deposit	meeting	balance	withdrawal
3	well	better	neatly	accurately
4	president	senator	tenant	mayor
5	tenth	six	fourth	twentieth
6	mail	send	fax	customer
7	louder	quicker	more	faster
8	dancer	hotel	typist	painter
9	allowed	permitted	don't	okay

B. Listen

Listen and choose the correct response.

1. a. I suppose not.
   b. Thank you.

2. a. I really appreciate it.
   b. I think so, too.

3. a. Are you sure?
   b. Does it?

4. a. Yes, we do.
   b. Yes, we are.

5. a. Please withdraw it.
   b. Please endorse it.

6. a. I don't know.
   b. How much is it?

7. a. Certainly.
   b. Not at all.

8. a. Oh? Why not?
   b. Didn't you?

9. a. I didn't believe.
   b. What happened?

10. a. Yes, you do.
    b. Yes, you are.

11. a. I think so.
    b. I'm a fish.

12. a. Nothing.
    b. You're right.

13. a. Please fix my sink.
    b. That's a good idea.

14. a. There is a law!
    b. They did a law!

15. a. You're welcome.
    b. Why?

C. What's the Word?

Complete the sentences.

quiet	quieter	quietest

good	better	best

1. This fan is ____quieter____ than that one.

2. We need a _____ fan.

3. They bought the _____ fan.

4. It's very _____.

5. It's _____ than that one.

6. It's the _____ one.

77

D. Fill It In!

Fill in the correct answer.

1 We _____ clean the house.
   a. has to
   (b.) have to

2 I _____ pay my bills.
   a. should
   b. not

3 She teaches very _____.
   a. good
   b. well

4 I can _____ the paychecks.
   a. set up
   b. give out

5 I'm sorry. They _____ work overtime.
   a. won't be able to
   b. don't do

6 She poked _____ in the eye.
   a. herself
   b. himself

7 She _____ on the wrong side of the road.
   a. did driving
   b. was driving

8 I'm sorry that I _____ come in early.
   a. shouldn't
   b. couldn't

9 Please _____ the check.
   a. endorse
   b. to endorse

10 It's _____ rain on Sunday.
   a. going to
   b. will

11 I'll give _____ the letter right now.
   a. them
   b. they

12 You're a very _____ dancer.
   a. gracefully
   b. graceful

13 Do you want me to _____ the sign?
   a. take down
   b. give out

14 My doctor says I _____ eat rich desserts.
   a. must
   b. musn't

15 They _____ fax the memo.
   a. wasn't able to
   b. weren't able to

16 Tenants _____ to put flowerpots there.
   a. aren't permit
   b. aren't permitted

17 You _____ write to the governor.
   a. ought to
   b. should to

18 Please try to work _____.
   a. good
   b. faster

E. What's the Verb?

Write the past form of the verb.

1 pay ___paid___   **4** make _____   **7** write _____

2 buy _____   **5** say _____   **8** try _____

3 forget _____   **6** hang up _____   **9** cut _____

A. What's the Word?

Complete the conversation.

| you | I | she | her | me |

A. Hello. ____I____ **1**'m Mr. Bennett.

B. Oh! Jane's father! _____ **2**'m pleased to meet _____ **3**.

A. Nice meeting _____ **4**, too. Tell _____ **5**, how is Jane doing in Science this year?

B. _____ **6**'s doing very well. _____ **7** works very hard, and _____ **8** grades are excellent. _____ **9** should be very proud of _____ **10**.

A. _____ **11**'m happy to hear that. Thank you.

B. Matching Lines

What extracurricular activities do these people do?

_h_ **1** Barbara sings every day.

____ **2** Tom is in the school play.

____ **3** Carol is the class president.

____ **4** Eric likes sports.

____ **5** Alice plays the violin.

____ **6** Paul is a "literary type."

____ **7** Janet plays the trombone.

____ **8** Carla likes to study languages.

____ **9** Fred loves to study plants and animals.

a. She's in the school band.

b. He's editor of the yearbook.

c. She's in the Spanish Club.

d. He's in the drama club.

e. She's in the orchestra.

f. He's on the baseball team.

g. He's involved in the Science Club.

h. She's in the school choir.

i. She's active in the student government.

C. What's the Word?

Complete the sentences.

I	you	he	she	we	they
my	your	his	her	our	their
me	you	him	her	us	them

1 We do very well in Spelling. It's ___our___ favorite subject. _____ parents are very proud of _____.

2 Libby loves Math. _____ grades are excellent. _____ loves to do Math homework.

3 Martha and Matt think Science is very interesting. _____ study Science every day. It's _____ best subject.

4 Juan works very hard in school. History is _____ best subject. _____ enjoys learning about the presidents.

5 I enjoy studying languages. This year _____'m studying French. It's _____ easiest subject, and it's _____ favorite subject.

6 Bill and Bob Bentley love Physical Education. _____ go to the gym every day. Football is _____ favorite sport.

D. Listen

What are they talking about? Listen and circle the correct answer.

1 History   (French and Spanish)   **5** Mathematics   yearbook

2 student government   literary magazine   **6** Spelling   school orchestra

3 football game   student government   **7** Science   tennis team

4 school choir   Physical Education   **8** drama club   school band

A. Wrong Way!

Put the lines in the correct order.

____ She is?

____ This is Mr. Park, the school guidance counselor, calling.

____ You're welcome. Good-bye.

_1_ Hello?

____ I'm afraid she is.

____ Yes?

____ Hello. Is this Mrs. Brown?

____ Lynn is cutting some of her classes.

____ Yes, it is.

____ All right. I promise I'll speak to her about this when she gets home. Thank you for letting me know.

B. Matching Lines

Match the lines.

_g_ **1** "We want your son to play on the soccer team."

____ **2** "We're having a meeting about college plans next week."

____ **3** "I'll turn on the heat soon."

____ **4** "Did you study for the grammar test?"

____ **5** "Be careful! Don't cut yourselves in this Science class!"

____ **6** "Linda has to play her trombone every day."

____ **7** "Your children are coming to school late every day."

____ **8** "Louis has a fever. Can you come to school and pick him up?"

a. Music teacher

b. homeroom teacher

c. Biology teacher

d. school nurse

e. English teacher

f. guidance counselor

g. coach

h. custodian

Decide Which Items Belong to People

A. The Right Choice

Circle the correct word.

1
A. Whose skis are these? Are they (us   **ours**)?
B. No. They aren't (our   ours). I think they're Bill and (Carol   Carol's).
A. Gee, I don't think so. (Theirs   Their) are older.
B. I'll ask (theirs   them).

A. Whose notebook computer is this? Is it (yours   your)?
B. No. It isn't (me   mine). I think it's (Jane's   Janes).
A. Gee, I don't think so. (Her   Hers) is more powerful.
B. I'll ask (her   hers).

3
A. Whose jacket is this? Is it (your   yours)?
B. No. It isn't (my   mine). I think it's (Jim's   Jim).
A. Gee, I don't think so. (His   He) is fancier.
B. I'll ask (his   him).

4
A. Whose kittens are these? Are they (yours   your)?
B. No. They aren't (my   mine). I think they're the (neighbors'   neighbor).
A. Gee, I don't think so. (Theirs   Their) are cuter.
B. I'll ask (him   them).

B. WordRap: *Whose Things?*

Listen. Then clap and practice.

A. Whose dog is this? Is it Jim's?
B. No, it's not. It's Tim's.
A. Whose gloves are these? Are they Jack's?
B. No, they're not. They're Mack's.
A. Whose coat is this? Is it Ann's?
B. No, it's not. It's Fran's.
A. Whose rings are these? Are they Ellen's?
B. No, they're not. They're Helen's.

ALL: Whose things? Whose things?
Whose things? Whose things?

Ask How Long People Will Be Busy

Student Text
Pages
136–137

A. The Right Choice

Circle the correct answer.

A. How much longer will you be studying?

B. (We'll be studying)ᴵ   until ²   another hour.
   We'll studying   for

A. How much longer will I be staying here in the hospital?

B. You be staying ³   until ⁴   the end of the week.
   You'll be staying   for

A. How much longer will Grandpa be sleeping?

B. He'll be sleeping ⁵   until ⁶   this program is over.
   He's sleeping   for

B. What's the Question?

Complete the questions.

1 A. How much longer __will you be watching this program__ ?
   B. I'll be watching this program until 10 o'clock.

2 A. How much longer _____ ?
   B. They'll be vacuuming for fifteen more minutes.

3 A. How much longer _____ ?
   B. He'll be playing ball until the school bus comes.

4 A. How much longer _____ ?
   B. She'll be practicing the violin until her violin teacher arrives.

5 A. How much longer _____ ?
   B. It'll be snowing for a few more hours.

A. What's the Response?

Choose the correct response.

1 What's new with you?
   a. Not much. How about you?
   b. I'm new?

2 I just won $50,000 in the lottery!
   a. That's great!
   b. I'm sorry to hear that.

3 I have some good news and some bad news. Which do you want to hear first?
   a. Pretty good.
   b. The good news.

4 Our neighbors sold their house for a lot of money.
   a. That's great!
   b. Are they upset?

5 Congratulations!
   a. What's the bad news?
   b. Thank you.

6 I have some good news.
   a. Really? What's good news?
   b. Really? What is it?

7 My husband got fired last week!
   a. That's too bad.
   b. Congratulations!

8 My wife and I are going to be getting a divorce, and my children are upset about it.
   a. I hope you can work it out.
   b. What's the bad news?

9 It's going to rain for three days.
   a. That's too bad.
   b. What is it?

10 My daughter is cutting classes every day, and she isn't doing her homework.
   a. That's wonderful!
   b. That's terrible!

B. What's the Answer?

Complete the answers.

1 Are you going to get a raise this year?   Yes, _____ I am _____.

2 Was Marie promoted?   Yes, _____.

3 Does your house have termites?   No, _____.

4 Did Mr. Grinchly raise your rent again?   Yes, _____.

5 Did Harry get another speeding ticket?   Yes, _____.

6 Are you going to have a baby?   No, _____.

7 Are your children upset you're going to be transferred?   Yes, _____.

A. Wrong Way!

Put the lines in the correct order.

___ No. What?

_1_ Did you hear the news?

___ The neighbors told me.

___ No kidding! Where did you hear that?

___ Our apartment building is going to be sold.

B. What's the Word?

Complete the sentences.

| problems | baby | hurricane | promoted | strike | divorce | broke up | arrested |

1 The government is having very bad financial ____problems____.

2 Did you hear the news? The man in Apartment 5 just got _____ by the police.

3 My sister is going to have a _____.

4 My supervisor and his wife are getting a _____.

5 Your secretary is going to be _____.

6 The city bus drivers are going on _____.

7 There's going to be a _____ this week.

8 Tim and Jennifer _____.

C. Sense or Nonsense?

Do the following "make sense" or are they "nonsense"?

	Sense	Nonsense
1 I read it on the radio.	_____	✓
2 Someone saw it on the 6 o'clock news.	_____	_____
3 I overheard it in the newspaper.	_____	_____
4 My next door neighbor told me.	_____	_____
5 All the radios are whispering about it.	_____	_____

D. What's the Word?

Complete the following. You decide what the rumor was.

announcement	company	overheard	rumor
cafeteria	conference	whispering	read

Bob heard a _____rumor_____ ¹ at work last Monday.
The whole _____ ² was talking about it.
The secretaries were _____ ³ about it in the
_____ ⁴. Bob _____ ⁵ two custodians
talking about it in the hallway. And Bob's supervisor
_____ ⁶ about it on his e-mail. Was the rumor
true? Finally, the company directors said, "We're going
to make an important _____ ⁷ at 4:00 P.M.
in the _____ ⁸ room." Everybody went and
listened. The rumor was true! The company directors
announced, "..

....

...."

E. Crosswalk

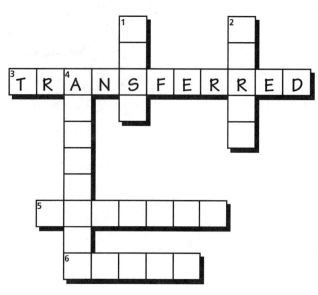

ACROSS

3 I'm going to be _____ to another
city and my family is upset about it.

5 I'm afraid your son _____ a fight
in the cafeteria.

6 Kathy isn't _____ her homework.

DOWN

1 I'm upset! I _____ fifty cents in
the vending machine.

2 My husband got _____ from
his job.

4 My son wasn't _____ to medical
school.

A. The Right Choice

Circle the correct word.

1
I really like your new sofa.
It's very ((colorful) intelligent).

Thank you.

(Where   When) did you get it?

I got it last weekend.

2
I really like your new puppy.
He's very (old   cute).

Thanks.

(What   Why) did you name him?

I named him Rusty.

3
I really like your new sports car.
It's very (flattering   smooth).

I agree.

(Why   When) did you get it?

I got it because
I'm going through
a mid-life crisis.

4
I like your new computer.
It's very (comfortable   powerful).

I know.

(Where   Why) did you buy it?

I bought it at
Computerland.

B. Matching Lines

Match the questions and answers.

_d_ **1** When did you buy it?

____ **2** How much does it weigh?

____ **3** Who cut your son's hair?

____ **4** What did you name your kitten?

____ **5** Why did you buy a motorcycle?

____ **6** Where did you get this sofa?

a. Sam at Supercuts Salon.

b. At Dave's Discount Department Store.

c. Because I really wanted one.

d. Last weekend.

e. Fluffy.

f. Two pounds.

A. The Right Choice

Circle the correct word.

A. [Who / **What**]¹ are you going to do on your next vacation?

B. I'm not [know / sure]². I'll probably go to the mountains. How about you?

A. I don't [sure / know]³. I [might / maybe]⁴ go to the beach, or I [might / maybe]⁵ stay home and relax.

B. Well, [whenever / whatever]⁶ you decide to do, I hope you enjoy yourself.

A. Thanks. [Me / You]⁷, too.

B. Listen

Listen and choose the correct answer.

1. a. She's going skiing.
    b. She might go skiing. ◯

2. a. It's going to be nice.
    b. The weather might be bad this weekend.

3. a. He's going skydiving.
    b. He might go skydiving.

4. a. They might retire.
    b. They're going to live in Houston when they retire.

5. a. He isn't going to watch the news.
    b. He might watch the news.

6. a. Maybe she'll work at the bank.
    b. She'll be working at the bank.

7. a. Maybe they'll go on vacation.
    b. They're going on vacation.

8. a. He's going to college when he finishes high school.
    b. He might go to college when he finishes high school.

C. Sure or Not Sure?

Are the speakers "sure" or "not sure"?

		Sure	Not Sure
1	"I might go to a movie this weekend."	_____	✓
2	"I know I'm going to get fired."	_____	_____
3	"You aren't allowed to stand there."	_____	_____
4	"The Robinsons are going to Florida soon."	_____	_____
5	"I think it might rain tomorrow."	_____	_____
6	"I'll be working here until the end of June."	_____	_____
7	"They don't know."	_____	_____
8	"I'm positive I'm going to the senior class picnic."	_____	_____
9	"Hmm. I think I'll do my homework today. But maybe I'll go to the beach. I really don't know."	_____	_____

D. The Right Choice

Circle the correct word.

1. Dan is doing very well in school. You (might (should)) be proud of him.
   We are.

2. It's going to rain this Saturday.
   We (might   must) have to cancel the senior class picnic.

3. When you make a long-distance call, you (might   have to) dial "zero."
   Oh. Thank you for telling me.

4. I have a terrible stomachache.
   Well, you (shouldn't   might) eat so many cookies.

5. You (mustn't   must) leave those garbage bags in the hallway.
   Oh. Sorry.

6. I'm upset about the pollution in our city.
   You (can't   ought to) write a letter to the newspaper.

Exit 8

Learn How to Politely Interrupt Someone

Student Text Pages 148–149

A. The Right Choice

Circle the correct word.

A. Excuse me. I'm **worry** / (**sorry**) to interrupt, but we need some more rice.

B. Did you say **ice** / **rice** ?

A. No. **Ice** / **Rice** .

B. Oh, okay. Thank you.

B. Listen

Listen and put a check next to the sentence you hear.

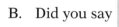 ✔ Always do your best!
___ Always wear your vest!

6 ___ You need to take these pills.
___ You need to take these bills.

2 ___ Do you have the time?
___ Do you have a dime?

7 ___ I'd like some juice.
___ I'd like some fruit.

3 ___ Is there any pepper in the soup?
___ Is there any butter in the soup?

8 ___ Make a turn at the right.
___ Make a turn at the light.

4 ___ Please put the bed near the table.
___ Please put the bread on the table.

9 ___ What was I doing wrong?
___ What was I doing for so long?

5 ___ Could you tell me where the kitchen is?
___ Could you tell me where the chicken is?

10 ___ I'm sorry, but that isn't correct.
___ I'm sorry, but that isn't collect.

C. Sense or Nonsense?

Do the following "make sense" or are they "nonsense"?

		Sense	Nonsense
1	"I like to go to the peach."	_____	✓
2	"I like to go to the beach."	_____	_____
3	"Please collect if I'm wrong."	_____	_____
4	"Please correct me if I'm wrong."	_____	_____
5	"These fries are delicious!"	_____	_____
6	"These ties are delicious!"	_____	_____
7	"Is he your cousin?"	_____	_____
8	"Is he your dozen?"	_____	_____
9	"This bathrobe is too tall."	_____	_____
10	"This bathrobe is too small."	_____	_____

D. Open Road!

Complete the conversations with words that sound the same.

1.
   A. Excuse me. I'm sorry to interrupt, . . .
      but the library closes at eight.
   B. Did you say ....late........?
   A. No. Eight. The library closes at eight.

A. Excuse me, Joe. I'm sorry to interrupt, . . .
   but there's a problem with the kitchen floor.
B. Did you say ....?
A. No. The floor.
B. Okay. I'll be there right away.

3.
   A. Excuse me, Henry. I'm sorry to interrupt, . . .
      but the boss wants to see you.
   B. Did you say ....?
   A. No. The boss.
   B. Okay. I'll go to his office right away.

A. Excuse me. I'm sorry to interrupt, . . .
   but Larry just hurt himself.
B. Did you say ....?
A. No. Larry.
B. Okay. I'll call the doctor.

Ask for and Give Clarification

A. What Does That Mean?

Circle true or false.

1 *Our computers are down.* — That means the computers are in the basement. — True — (False)

2 *She threw in the towel.* — That means she quit. — True — False

3 *We're overbooked.* — That means there are books on all the seats. — True — False

4 *This is my treat.* — That means she's going to eat all the cake. — True — False

5 *The test results are negative.* — That means the test results are good. — True — False

6 *I'll give you a ring.* — That means he'll stop by to visit. — True — False

B. Listen

Where are they? Listen to the conversation and check the place.

1 ✔ in a park
___ in an office

2 ___ in a restaurant
___ at a lake

3 ___ in a gym
___ in a bank

4 ___ at an airport
___ at a train station

5 ___ in a doctor's office
___ in a school

6 ___ in a school
___ in a bakery

7 ___ at a concert
___ in a school

8 ___ in an office
___ in someone's house

A. Matching Lines

Match the lines.

_e_ **1** It looks like a storm is coming.

____ **2** Our English teacher taught us a lot.

____ **3** The boss is in a terrible mood today.

____ **4** This movie isn't very good.

____ **5** The children don't look very healthy.

____ **6** You take too many vitamins.

____ **7** Bruce and Brenda will break up soon.

____ **8** Those pies look very good!

a. I agree. They don't.

b. I agree. They will.

c. I agree. She did.

d. I agree. She is.

e. I agree. It does.

f. I agree. They do.

g. I agree. It isn't.

h. I agree. I do.

B. What's the Response?

Choose the correct response.

1 The soup doesn't taste very good.
    (a.) You're right. It's cold.
    b. I know. It's in a terrible mood.

2 We should take the bus to work.
    a. I agree. The bus is very
       crowded today.
    b. You're right. The expressway
       is very crowded.

3 Our children should go to college.
    a. I agree. They shouldn't.
    b. You're right. They're very
       intelligent.

4 The mayor is in a terrible mood.
    a. I know. We probably shouldn't
       bother him.
    b. You're right. We should bother
       him.

5 Sam makes delicious chicken!
    a. I agree. I'd like his recipe.
    b. You're right. It tastes terrible.

6 We should have a party for our
teacher.
    a. You're right. She doesn't look
       very healthy.
    b. I know. She taught us a lot.

7 There's going to be a hurricane soon.
    a. I know. We should leave the
       beach now.
    b. Okay. Let's go swimming.

8 Cutting classes isn't allowed at this
school.
    a. Okay. Let's go home now.
    b. I know. Everybody has to go to
       class.

Learn Ways to Disagree with Someone

Student Text
Pages
154–155

A. Wrong Way!

Put the lines in the correct order.

____ He smiles at you all the time. Don't you agree?

____ Oh? Why do you say that?

_1_ You know . . . I think the new student likes you.

____ No, not really. I disagree.

B. Matching Lines

Match the lines.

_d_ **1** Yesterday's test was a piece of cake.

____ **2** Well, I think it's time to hit the books.

____ **3** The food in the restaurant is terrible!

____ **4** Everybody says this new CD is very hot.

____ **5** I think this TV program is very interesting.

____ **6** It's much too warm in the office today.

____ **7** In my opinion, Gregory is a wonderful singer.

____ **8** I think we should brainstorm right now.

a. I disagree. I think it's too cold in here.

b. Gee, I hear it isn't very popular at all!

c. I disagree. I don't think he's talented at all!

d. I disagree. I thought it was difficult.

e. I disagree. We can think about it later.

f. I disagree. I think it's boring.

g. I disagree. We can study later.

h. I disagree. I think it's delicious.

94

C. What's the Word?

Complete the conversations.

efficient	mood	stale	creamy	fading	nervous	strange	relaxed

1 I think I'll try meditation. I'm very ___nervous___ .

2 I think these cookies are _____. They're very hard.

3 This car isn't very safe. It's making _____ noises.

4 I think this yogurt tastes just like ice cream. It's very rich and _____.

5 I think we should buy a new TV. The colors on our TV are _____.

6 The Johnsons are on vacation. They're very _____.

7 I'm in a wonderful _____ today. I just got a big promotion!

8 Janet is probably going to get fired from her job. She isn't a very _____ worker.

D. Open Road!

Do you agree or disagree with the following statements?

I agree.	You're right.	I know.	I disagree.

1 "Our English class is very interesting." ....

2 "Our classmates speak English very well." ....

3 "Students should express their opinions in class." ....

4 "Students ought to study every day." ....

5 "The students in our class like to study English." ....

Say Good-Bye to Someone

A. The Right Choice

Circle the correct word.

A. By the way, what ((time) dime)**1** is it?

B. It's 4:00.

A. Oh! It's late! I've really (have to   got to)**2** go now. I (got to   have to)**3** get to class.

B. Okay. See you soon.

A. Good-bye.

A. You know, I think I should be going now. I've (got to   have to)**4** be home before dark.

B. I (could   should)**5** be going, too.

A. So (wrong   long)**6**.

B. See you (soon   noon)**7**.

B. More Right Choices

Circle the correct word.

1 I've really got to go now. I have to pick up my husband (in   (at)) 6:00 P.M.

2 You'll have your test results (by   in) a few minutes.

3 My homework will be finished (in   at) half an hour.

4 I've got to get to the supermarket (by   before) it closes.

5 I have to get to the doctor (by   in) 4:00.

6 Can you please call back (in   at) an hour?

7 I have to finish washing my car (before   by) it rains.

8 Your advisor will meet with you (before   in) fifteen minutes.

9 Marty saw the red light (at   before) I did.

10 Somebody got fired. I heard it (in   before) the cafeteria.

96

C. Listen

Listen and put a check next to the best way to finish the conversation.

1 ✔ It's 3:15.
___ It's Monday.

2 ___ Go?
___ Okay. See you soon.

3 ___ Good-bye.
___ Yes, you can.

4 ___ I agree.
___ Anything else?

5 ___ Thank you for saying so.
___ So long.

6 ___ Okay. Take care.
___ I'm sorry.

7 ___ Oh. That's nice.
___ Okay. I'll talk to you soon.

8 ___ Okay. Take it easy.
___ You're wrong.

9 ___ I really appreciate it.
___ No, not really. I disagree.

10 ___ Yes, I can.
___ All right. Good-bye.

D. Word Search

Find 6 ways of saying "good-bye."

```
D O N Z W (S O L O N G) S E E T T E O P
V T A K K E E Y U O I Y C A L Y I N T
D G Y B C Z W P L K J S O O N O N T A
J T K V Y U B M Z T A K E X N U I N K
T A K S C U C A L Y O J T B D J R P E
B K Y I O N C G O O D J Y V P A S S C
M E D T O U I N M A B X Z B Y I N P A
W I T C Y I P C A L L E T Y O G U J R
R T U A L R U G O O D B Y E U K B B E
S E S L O G G U S O T T Y U S U I Y U
E A E M N Y H O S U L E W S O A S Y R
E S E S H N T J V J R U G S O L O Y C
D Y I C O S E E Y O U S O O N E L T Y
Q G T V M K E S H D F G G H E Y O U I
```

97

Exchange Opinions

A. Wrong Way!

Put the lines in the correct order.

____ No, not really. I disagree. In my opinion, the chocolate shakes at Ray Roger's are more delicious.

____ Well, I'm not so sure. Why so you say that?

____ Oh? What makes you say that?

__1__ You know . . . I think the chocolate shakes at Burger Town taste better than the ones at Ray Roger's.

____ Hmm. Maybe you're right.

____ The chocolate shakes at Burger Town are sweeter. Don't you think so?

____ The chocolate shakes at Ray Roger's are more refreshing.

B. Fill It In!

Fill in the correct answer.

1 In my opinion, English is a very difficult language to learn because the spelling isn't ____.
   (a.) easy
   b. always

2 In my opinion, English is an easy language to learn because the grammar rules ____ difficult.
   a. are
   b. aren't

3 I really don't like popular music today. In my opinion, all the songs are ____.
   a. wonderful
   b. boring

4 I think today's popular music is wonderful. In my opinion, all the songs are ____.
   a. exciting
   b. terrible

5 Too much of our paycheck goes to the government. I think our taxes are too ____.
   a. low
   b. high

6 I disagree. The government needs our tax dollars. ____ our taxes are high at all.
   a. I think
   b. I don't think

7 Saving money is difficult today because ____ too many bills to pay.
   a. there are
   b. there aren't

8 I don't agree. I think it's easy to save money today because the price of food is so ____.
   a. high
   b. low

C. Listen

Listen and put a check next to the best way to finish the conversation.

1 ✔ Fine, thanks. And you?
___ I have a terrible headache.

2 ___ Fine, thanks. And you?
___ I have a bad cold.

3 ___ No. I think they're wrong.
___ I'm not really sure.

4 ___ Hi. How are you?
___ Good-bye.

5 ___ I agree. It's great.
___ You're wrong. It's great.

6 ___ Okay. Good-bye.
___ How are you?

7 ___ Are you sure?
___ Okay. Bye.

8 ___ So long.
___ Hello.

9 ___ I agree.
___ You're welcome.

10 ___ See you soon.
___ You're right. It's easy.

D. The 5th Wheel!

Which one doesn't belong?

1 I know. | You're wrong. | You're right. | I agree.
2 I disagree. | I know. | I'm not sure. | Why do you say that?
3 It did? | It isn't? | It wasn't? | It won't?
4 boss | computer | secretary | office assistant
5 History | football team | drama club | yearbook
6 coach | principal | father | guidance counselor

E. WordRap: *Saying Good-Bye*

Listen. Then clap and practice.

A. It's getting late.
  I've got to fly.
  I've got to run.
B. Good-bye. Good-bye.

A. I've got to go.
  It's almost noon.
  I've got to leave.
B. See you soon!

A. It's time to leave.
  I have to go.
  It's getting late.
B. I know. I know.

A. What's the Word?

Complete the sentences.

my	us	your	you're	their	it	we	him

1 In ___my___ opinion, it's correct.

2 Children need _____ parents.

3 What's _____ favorite subject?

4 What do _____ do?

5 Let's give _____ a promotion.

6 I know _____ going to disagree.

7 We want our raise. Give it to _____.

8 Take _____ easy.

B. Matching Lines

Match the questions and answers.

_b_ **1** Is this the boys' ball?   a. Yes, it's ours.

___ **2** Is this Jim's book?   b. Yes, it's theirs.

___ **3** Is this our car?   c. No, it isn't yours.

___ **4** Is this Mom's coat?   d. No, it isn't hers.

___ **5** Is this mine?   e. Yes, it's his.

C. What's the Response?

Write the correct response.

1 Is he doing well in school?

Yes, _____he is_____.

2 Do your children do well in Math?

Yes, _____.

3 Will she take a shower after gym?

No, _____.

4 Will you be here until noon?

Yes, _____.

5 Does he have any good news?

Yes, _____.

6 Is this your treat?

Yes, _____.

7 Did they play on the football team?

No, _____.

8 Was he in the school band?

Yes, _____.

9 Are taxes too high?

Yes, _____.

10 Did you get fired?

Yes, _____.

11 Did you and Bill hear the news?

No, _____.

12 Do you have any more questions?

No, _____.

D. Listen

Listen and choose the correct response.

1   a. I'm happy to hear that.   **4**   a. I'm happy to hear that.   **7**   a. I'm sorry to hear that.
     b. I'm sorry to hear that.   b. I'm sorry to hear that.   b. I'm happy to hear that.

2   a. That's great!   **5**   a. That's great!   **8**   a. That's great!
     b. I'm sorry to hear that.   b. That's too bad!   b. That's terrible!

3   a. Congratulations!   **6**   a. Congratulations!   **9**   a. That's wonderful!
     b. That's too bad!   b. I'm sorry to hear that.   b. That's terrible!

E. The Right Choice

Circle the correct word.

1
When
What   did they break up?
Who

4
Who
Why   got promoted?
When

2
Who
What   much longer will you be here?
How

5
What
Where   are you going tonight?
Which

3
When
What   did you do last night?
Where

6
Who
Which   is the plane overbooked?
Why

F. Matching Lines

Match the lines.

_d_   **1**   I think we should be going now.

___   **2**   Do you agree?

___   **3**   What can I do to relax?

___   **4**   What's your favorite subject?

___   **5**   How did you hear about the strike?

___   **6**   How much longer will he be on the phone?

a. You can try meditation.

b. For another half hour.

c. My neighbor told me.

d. But we just got here!

e. History.

f. No, I disagree.

Page 3

Listen and circle the word you hear.

1. You can't leave your garbage here.
2. Your brother can play here with his friends.
3. You can park your car in front of the building.
4. We can't hang our laundry on the balcony.
5. You can plant a garden in back of the building.
6. You can use the fireplace.
7. The superintendent can't come to the apartment now.
8. You can't play music after 11 P.M.
9. I can't go to the movies with you on Saturday.

Page 4

Listen and circle the word you hear.

1. A. Can I help you take out the garbage?
   B. No. That's okay. I can take it out myself.
2. A. Please hang up your laundry right now.
   B. Okay, Mom. But I can't do it by myself.
3. A. Did you put away the tables and chairs?
   B. Yes. I put them away this morning.
4. A. Can we help you clean up this mess?
   B. No, that's okay. I can clean it up myself.
5. A. Did they cut down your trees on Monday?
   B. No. They cut them down this morning.
6. A. Can you pick up those heavy bags for me?
   B. Certainly. I can pick them up for you right now.
7. A. You should put your things away.
   B. I know. I'm going to put them away right now.
8. A. Excuse me. Can I help you carry those bags?
   B. No. That's okay. I can carry them myself.
9. A. Did your husband take out the garbage?
   B. Yes. He took it out this morning.

Page 5

Listen and decide what these people are talking about.

1. Here. Let me help you carry them.
2. Thank you, but I can clean it up myself.

3. I can help you cut it down.
4. Here. I can help you take it out.
5. I can help you put them away.
6. Can I help you pick them up?

Page 7

Listen and circle the word you hear.

1. We rang your doorbell yesterday, but you weren't at home.
2. Do you have a car?
3. Bill was at school all day today.
4. On our vacation we drove through the Rocky Mountains.
5. Can you come to dinner on Friday?
6. Where did you go?
7. The Millers want to see a movie tonight.
8. I heard about the big storm on the radio.
9. Grandma and Grandpa called us this morning.
10. We were at Disneyland last week.
11. Please stop by for a visit.
12. We took the bus to Washington.
13. Do you baby-sit?
14. We went to Chicago last year.
15. You weren't in school this morning.
16. I read it in the newspaper today.

Page 9

Listen to the conversation and choose the correct answer.

A. What are you doing?
B. I'm trying to fix this radiator.
A. What's wrong with it?
B. It doesn't get hot.
A. I see. And you're trying to fix it yourself?
B. Yes. And I'm having a lot of trouble.
A. You know, maybe you should call a plumber.
B. Hmm. You're probably right.

Page 11

Listen and decide what these people are talking about.

1. It's leaking. I'm going to call a plumber.
2. It doesn't flush. We should call a plumber.
3. It doesn't get hot. Maybe we should call the superintendent.
4. We can't cook dinner because it doesn't go on. I'm going to call the gas company.
5. It doesn't close. I'm going to call a carpenter.
6. It doesn't wash the dishes. We should call a plumber.
7. We can't drive it. We should call a mechanic.
8. It doesn't get cold. We should call the superintendent.

Page 14

Listen to the conversation. Check the directions you hear.

1. A. Excuse me. Could you tell me how to make a collect call?
   B. Sure. Dial "zero." Then, dial the area code and the local number. Tell the operator it's a collect call and give your name. Have you got that?
   A. I think so. I dial "zero." Then, I dial the area code and the local number. And then I . . . hmm. Could you repeat the last step?
   B. Yes. Tell the operator it's a collect call and give your name.
   A. Okay. I understand. Thanks very much.
2. A. Excuse me. Could you tell me how to use this pay phone?
   B. Sure. Pick up the receiver. Put the money in the coin slot. Then, dial the number. Have you got that?
   A. I think so. Let me see. I pick up the receiver. I put the money in the coin slot. And then I dial the number.
3. A. Excuse me. Could you tell me how to make a person-to-person call?
   B. Sure. Dial "zero." Dial the area code and the local phone number. Tell the operator it's a person-to-person call and give the name of the person you're calling. Have you got that?
   A. I think so. I dial "zero." Then, I dial the area code and the local number. And then I . . . hmm. Could you repeat the last step?
   B. Yes. Tell the operator it's a person-to-person call and give the name of the person you're calling.
   A. Okay. I understand. Thanks very much.

Page 15

Listen and put a check next to the sentence you hear.

1. Is this Lally's Department Store?
2. Do you have any peaches?
3. Did you call at seven?
4. I fixed the train.
5. Is the museum open late?
6. I think you're right.
7. The collect call was from my brother.
8. Do you sell pears?
9. Is your name Hal?
10. Are you calling Mr. Reardon?
11. They sell gold watches.
12. What's the address on the door?
13. Please come and see.
14. Is there a problem with your earring?

Page 18
Listen and complete the train schedule.

1. The train to Atlanta leaves at 11:05 A.M.
2. A round-trip ticket to Philadelphia is $78.60.
3. The one-way fare to New York is $37.50.
4. The train to Philadelphia leaves at 4:37 P.M.
5. The one-way fare to Atlanta is $64.80.
6. A round-trip ticket to Washington is $90.75.

Page 26
Listen and circle the food item you hear.

1. A. May I help you?
   B. Yes, please. I'd like a jar of mustard.
2. A. Anything else?
   B. Yes. A pound of ground beef.
3. A. May I help you?
   B. Yes, please. I'd like a pint of chocolate ice cream.
4. A. Anything else?
   B. Yes. Two loaves of white bread.
5. A. May I help you?
   B. Yes, please. Half a pound of Swiss cheese.
6. A. Anything else?
   B. Yes. A pound of potato salad.
7. A. May I help you?
   B. Yes, please. I'd like three jars of mayonnaise.
8. A. Anything else?
   B. Yes. A bunch of grapes.
9. A. May I help you?
   B. Yes, please. Four pieces of chicken.
10. A. Anything else?
    B. Yes. Two dozen rolls.

Page 28
Listen and decide if the prices are "likely" or "unlikely."

1. A dozen hot dogs? That'll be seventeen cents.
2. A bag of potato chips? That's one twenty-nine.
3. A pound of chicken? That'll be seventy-nine dollars and ninety-nine cents.
4. A quart of milk? That'll be a dollar nineteen.
5. A jar of mustard? That'll be forty-seven fifty.
6. A dozen eggs? That'll be one cent.

Page 29
Listen and circle the correct answer.

1. I'd like a small order of . . .
2. I'll have a cup of . . .
3. I'd like two . . .
4. I'd like a roast beef . . .
5. I'd like two pieces of . . .
6. I'd like three containers of . . .

Page 30
Listen to the order and choose the correct item.

1. I'd like a large order of french fries.
2. I'll have a cup of coffee.
3. I'd like two tacos.
4. Three pieces of chicken, please.
5. I'll have an order of refried beans.
6. A chocolate shake, please.
7. I'd like a roast beef sandwich.
8. I'll have two fish sandwiches.
9. A medium Coke, please.
10. I'd like three cheeseburgers.

Page 32
Listen and circle the correct answer.

1. I'd like a glass of . . .
2. I'd prefer mashed . . .
3. I'd like lamb . . .
4. I'd like some iced . . .
5. Hmm. I think I'd like a baked . . .
6. I'm really thirsty. I'd like a . . .

Page 33
Listen and circle the correct answer.

1. Here. Have a little more . . . !
2. Do you want a few more . . . ?
3. Would you like a few more . . . ?
4. Come on! Have a little more . . . !

Page 35
Listen and put the recipe instructions in the correct order.

1. Welcome to the Friendly Gourmet Cooking Show! Today's recipe is for baked beans. First, mix together beans, onions, and ketchup. Then, put the mixture into a pan. Next, bake the mixture for four hours at 325 degrees. Serve the baked beans with hot dogs. You'll love them!
2. Welcome to the Friendly Gourmet Cooking Show! Today we're going to make orange cake. First, mix together a cup of flour, a little water, and a teaspoon of salt. Then, add a cup of sugar and a little orange juice. Next, add an egg. Put the mixture into a baking pan and bake for one hour at 350 degrees. You'll really like this orange cake!
3. Here's a wonderful recipe for mashed potatoes! First, cook the potatoes for twenty minutes. Then, mix the potatoes with a little milk and butter. Next, add a little salt and pepper. Serve with meat and vegetables.
4. Here's one of our favorite chicken recipes! First, put salt, pepper, garlic, and lemon all over the chicken. Then, put it on a rack in the oven. Next, bake it for one hour at 375 degrees. Serve it with baked potatoes and a salad. You'll really like this chicken recipe!

Page 38
Listen and circle the word you hear.

1. They bought a box of cookies.
2. I spent $10.00 at the store today.
3. I take the bus to Buffalo.
4. My husband and I sit in the park in the evening.
5. They rode on the train.
6. I had an apple for lunch.
7. We get home from work late.
8. Do the children wake up at 7:00?
9. They ate hot dogs for dinner.

Page 42
Listen to the advertisements and check the words you hear.

1. Buy a Magnabox TV! The picture on the Magnabox is the clearest and the brightest you can buy! Everybody agrees the Magnabox TV is the best!
2. Do you need a computer? Buy a McDougal today! The McDougal is more dependable than the MBI Computer. In fact, it's the most dependable and the most powerful computer you can buy. And the best news is that it's cheaper than the MBI!

Page 45
Listen and circle the word you hear.

1. I wrote a check to University Bookstore for the textbooks.
2. I'm going to balance the checkbook today.
3. Here's a check for one twenty-five.
4. Do you remember the amount?
5. I'd like to cash this thirteen dollar check.
6. I wrote a check to Sound Studio for CDs.
7. Here's a check to pay the credit card bill.
8. The check for this month's utilities is one sixty-two fifty.
9. Did you write a check for Bill's medicine?
10. Did you remember to sign the check?

Page 48
Marcia is very busy this month. There are a lot of dates in June she has to remember. Listen and write the number of each special occasion on Marcia's calendar.

1. Her son's birthday is on June 5th.
2. Her parents' anniversary is on the 7th.
3. Marcia's daughter's graduation is on the 11th.
4. Her son's graduation is on the 15th.
5. Marcia has to remember to buy a gift for her grandmother. Her 75th birthday is on June 19th.
6. Her grandfather's birthday is on the 23rd. He'll be 82 years old!

103

7. Marcia and her husband have a special anniversary this month. Their 25th anniversary is on June 26th.
8. To celebrate their anniversary, Marcia and her husband are going to take a vacation trip to Greece on the 30th. What a busy month!

Page 50

Listen to the conversations and choose the correct answer.

1. A. Is there a mistake on the check?
   B. Yes. The amount isn't correct.
2. A. What's the problem with your gas bill?
   B. I was charged too much.
3. A. Did you remember to check the balance of the checking account?
   B. Yes, I did. I used a calculator.
4. A. Do you have a monthly budget?
   B. Yes, I do.
5. A. Do you write your expenses in a notebook?
   B. Yes. I know exactly how much money I can add to my savings account every month.
6. A. When is the telephone bill due?
   B. It's due on the twentieth.
7. A. I'd like to cash this check, please.
   B. All right. Please endorse it and write your account number on the back.
8. A. What's the amount of the tuition bill?
   B. Five hundred and twenty-five dollars.
   A. Five hundred and twenty-five dollars?
   B. Yes.

Page 52

Listen and circle the correct answer.

1. A. Would you like me to take down the "sale" signs?
   B. Yes. Please take them down.
2. A. Could you please call Mr. Chen?
   B. Of course. I'll call him right away.
3. A. Could you put away these dishes, please?
   B. Okay. I'll put them away right now.
4. A. Billy, could you please clean up your bedroom?
   B. Okay, Mom. I'll clean it up in a few minutes.
5. A. Please give this report to the Board of Directors.
   B. Certainly. I'll give them the report right away.
6. A. I'll be happy to hang up these announcements.
   B. Thanks. Hang them up this morning.

Page 54

Who am I? Listen and circle the correct answer.

1. You can see me on TV. People like to watch me.
2. I work at a school.
3. I speak many languages, and I work at the United Nations.
4. I work in an office.
5. I work in a factory.
6. Sometimes I work outside, and sometimes I work inside.
7. I work in a restaurant.
8. I work in a garage.
9. People watch me in the movies.
10. I interview people.
11. I study at a university.
12. People call me when there's an emergency.

Page 58

Yesterday or tomorrow? Listen and circle the correct answer.

1. I wasn't able to work overtime. I had to take my son to the doctor.
2. Bill won't be able to work this weekend. He has to attend a wedding out of town.
3. I'm happy I'll be able to see your presentation.
4. I couldn't work late. I had to pick up my car from the mechanic.
5. Betty couldn't work because she was sick.
6. I'm sorry I won't be able to help you take inventory. I have to go to my son's soccer game.
7. I won't be able to come in early. I have to go to the dentist.
8. They couldn't come to the party. They had to work.
9. Won't you be able to come to the meeting?
10. I wasn't able to cook dinner. I had to stay at work and finish the annual report.
11. Charlie won't be able to unload the shipment of new clothing. He's having problems with his back.
12. I'll be able to attend the meeting.
13. We were able to stay until the end of the meeting.
14. I couldn't set up the conference room. I had to pick up my mother at the airport.

Page 61

Listen and circle the word you hear.

1. Be careful! You're going to spill hot cereal all over yourselves!
2. We spilled hot cereal on ourselves!
3. I cut myself!
4. She hurt herself on her machine.
5. We celebrated our anniversary by ourselves.
6. There's an accident on Fourth Street! A dog hurt itself!
7. The waiter cut himself!
8. Be careful! Don't poke yourself in the eye!
9. The children hurt themselves.

Page 64

Are you allowed to . . .? Listen and choose "Yes" or "No."

1. You aren't allowed to park in front of the hospital.
2. You can fish here.
3. You're not allowed to stand in front of the white line on the bus.
4. You're allowed to camp here.
5. You can park in front of the door.
6. They're having a meeting. You're not allowed to go in.
7. There's no smoking in the movie theater.
8. Food and drinks aren't allowed in the classrooms.
9. You can't swim here.

Page 68

Listen and put the number under the traffic violation you hear about.

Officer Burton gave five traffic tickets today at the corner of Oak and Main Streets.

1. The first car made an illegal U turn.
2. The second car drove through a stop sign.
3. The third car was driving on the wrong side of the road.
4. The fourth car was speeding.
5. And the fifth car went through a red light.

Officer Burton certainly had a busy day today!

Page 70

What are they talking about? Listen and circle the correct answer.

1. I'll turn it on this afternoon.
2. I already contacted Channel 5 News.
3. Are you going to clean it up soon?
4. We'll fix them soon.
5. I'm going to remove it soon.
6. We promise we'll take it out tonight.
7. I already repaired it.
8. I'll return it next week.
9. When are you going to paint them?
10. I promise I'll spray it tomorrow.

Page 73

Listen and choose the correct answer.

1. You must always . . .
2. You must never . . .
3. You mustn't . . .
4. You must always . . .
5. You mustn't forget to . . .
6. You must never . . .
7. You must always . . .
8. You mustn't . . .

Page 76

Listen to the conversations and choose the correct answer.

Conversation 1

A. Good evening. You're on WCDN Talk Radio.

B. I'm upset. In my opinion, the city should pick up the garbage every day.
A. Why do you say that?
B. There's too much garbage everywhere. It's a mess on the streets!
A. You should write to the Health Department. Also, you ought to call the mayor.
B. Those are good ideas. I will.

Conversation 2

A. I'm going to write to the president.
B. Why?
A. Cable TV is very expensive. In my opinion, it should be cheaper.
B. You ought to write to the newspaper, too. And you should send a letter to your congressman.
A. Those are good ideas! I will.

Page 77

Listen and choose the correct response.

1. I don't think we can afford it.
2. This apartment is really noisy!
3. Channel 8 is the best TV channel.
4. We have to stop at the bank.
5. I'd like to cash this check.
6. What's the problem?
7. Could you give this memo to Mr. Jackson?
8. I won't be able to work this weekend.
9. You won't believe what happened!
10. Am I working quickly enough?
11. Are you allowed to fish here?
12. What did I do wrong?
13. What can I do for you?
14. There ought to be a law!
15. Thanks for telling me.

Page 80

What are they talking about? Listen and circle the correct answer.

1. A. Susan is very smart.
   B. I know. She's taking two languages this year.
2. A. What extracurricular activity do you do?
   B. Me? I'm the "literary type."
3. A. Are you going to the meeting?
   B. Yes. I want to hear the new senior class president talk to the class.
4. A. Does Agnes enjoy singing?
   B. Yes. She sings every day at school.
5. A. Did Mr. Small help you with your homework?
   B. Yes. I'm not having any trouble with the numbers now.
6. A. Veronica plays the violin very well.
   B. Well, you know . . . she plays every day at school.

7. A. What's your favorite subject?
   B. Biology. I love to learn about plants and animals.
8. A. Did you see the new school play?
   B. Yes. There are many talented actors in this school.

Page 88

Listen and choose the correct answer.

1. A. What are you going to do over the holiday?
   B. I'm not sure. I'll probably go skiing.
2. A. What's the weather forecast for the weekend?
   B. It's going to be sunny and warm.
3. A. Are you really going skydiving?
   B. Yes, I am!
4. A. Where are you and your husband going to live when you retire?
   B. We'll definitely be living in Houston. Our children live there.
5. A. Are you going to watch the news on TV?
   B. Probably.
6. A. What's your daughter going to do this summer?
   B. She isn't sure. She might work at the bank.
7. A. What are Grandma and Grandpa going to do for their 50th wedding anniversary?
   B. They might go on vacation.
8. A. Will your son be going to college when he finishes high school?
   B. He doesn't know.

Page 90

Listen and put a check next to the sentence you hear.

1. My mother says, "Always do your best!"
2. Do you have a dime?
3. Is there any pepper in the soup?
4. Please put the bread on the table.
5. Could you tell me where the chicken is?
6. You need to take these pills.
7. I'd like some fruit.
8. Make a turn at the light.
9. What was I doing wrong?
10. I'm sorry, but that isn't correct.

Page 92

Where are they? Listen to the conversation and check the place.

1. It's raining cats and dogs. We should go inside.
2. I'm sorry, but we're out of fish.
3. I can't balance your account now. Our computers are down.
4. I'm sorry. The flight is overbooked.
5. Mr. Jones, I'm happy to tell you the tests were negative.

6. This test is a piece of cake!
7. Jimmy, you didn't do your homework.
8. I have to leave for the office now. I'll call you when I get home.

Page 97

Listen and put a check next to the best way to finish the conversation.

1. By the way, what time is it?
2. I've really got to go now.
3. See you soon.
4. This test was a piece of cake!
5. I think I should be going now. I've got to get to my next performance.
6. I'll call you soon.
7. I've got to hang up now. The bus is here.
8. Sorry. We have to leave right now.
9. The weather this week is terrible. Don't you agree?
10. You're late! You've got to leave right now!

Page 99

Listen and put a check next to the best way to finish the conversation.

1. Hi. How are you?
2. You know . . . you don't look very well.
3. I think the government is too big. Do you agree?
4. Hello.
5. This concert is very good.
6. I'll call you soon.
7. I've got to go now. I have to pick up my children at school.
8. Have a nice day.
9. Thank you.
10. Take it easy.

Page 101

Listen and choose the correct response.

1. You should be very proud of your daughter. She's the best student in the class.
2. Your son started a fight in school this morning.
3. I was just accepted to business school.
4. The boss is in a terrible mood today.
5. My husband got fired.
6. I won a laptop computer!
7. According to my doctor, all the tests were negative.
8. Our computers are down.
9. That test was a piece of cake!

CORRELATION
ExpressWays Student Text/ExpressWays Activity Workbook

Student Text Pages	Activity Workbook Pages	Student Text Pages	Activity Workbook Pages
Exit 1		**Exit 5**	
2–3	1	88–89	51
4–5	2	90–91	52–53
6–7	3	92–93	54–55
8–9	4–5	94–95	56–57
10–11	6	96–99	58–59
12–13	7–8	100–101	60–61
14–15	9–10	102–103	62–63
16–19	11–12		
		Exit 6	
Exit 2		106–109	64–65
22–25	13–14	110–111	66
26–27	15	112–113	67–68
28–31	16–17	114–115	69
32–35	18–19	116–117	70–71
36–37	20–21	118–119	72–73
38–41	22–23	120–123	74–76
Exit 3		**Exit 7**	
44–47	24–25	128–131	79–80
48–49	26–27	132–133	81
50–51	28	134–135	82
52–53	29–30	136–137	83
54–55	31–32	138–139	84
56–57	33–34	140–141	85–86
58–61	35–36	142–143	87
		144–145	88–89
Exit 4		**Exit 8**	
66–69	39–40	148–149	90–91
70–73	41–42	150–151	92
74–75	43	152–153	93
76–77	44	154–155	94–95
78–79	45	156–159	96–97
80–81	46	160–163	98–99
82–83	47–48		
84–85	49–50		